also from

aplomb publishing
San Francisco

Reel Horror - True Horrors Behind Hollywood's Scary Movies

Disaster in the Sky - Behind the Scenes of the Airport Movies

Curse of the Silver Screen - Tragedy & Disaster Behind the Movies

Master of Disaster - Irwin Allen: The Disaster Years

Diana Ross in Central Park - A 25th Anniversary Retrospective

Disaster on Film - Behind the Scenes of Hollywood's Classic Disaster Films

www.aplombpublishing.com

Alfred Hitchcock
•
The Icon Years

By John William Law

aplomb publishing
San Francisco

Alfred Hitchcock - The Icon Years

Published by Aplomb Publishing, San Francisco, California.
Copyright 2010.

978-0-9665676-4-9

1st edition

Manufactured in the United States of America.

About the cover: *Our cover was designed to represent Hitchcock, circa 1960, at the height his success and tied indelibly to his most famous motion picture, 'Psycho'. The Janet Leigh shower scream represents a struggle Hitchcock would carry through the remainder of his career to recapture the cinematic greatness of his most famous film.*

No part of this publication may be reprinted without written permission from the publisher. For more information, write Aplomb Publishing, editor@aplombpublishing.com.

Dedicated to my parents, David and Elizabeth Law,
who never quite understood my fascination
with old movies, but let me watch nonetheless.

"In the old days villains had moustaches and kicked the dog. Audiences are smarter today. They don't want their villain to be thrown at them with green limelight on his face. They want an ordinary human being with failings."

- Alfred Hitchcock

Table of Contents

1	introductory remarks	Page 13
2	the icon & the man	Page 21
3	the early years	Page 27
4	closing out the 50s	Page 35
5	no bail for the judge	Page 41
6	psycho	Page 51
7	the birds	Page 63
8	moma exhibition	Page 75
9	marnie	Page 81
10	the saga of mary rose	Page 93
11	torn curtain	Page 127
12	the auteur filmmaker	Page 141
13	topaz	Page 149
14	accolades & honors	Page 157
15	frenzy	Page 163
16	family plot	Page 175
17	the short night	Page 185
18	one last honor	Page 191
19	the end	Page 197
20	closing remarks	Page 203

Appendix

filmography	Page 211
sources	Page 217
index	Page 223

ALFRED HITCHCOCK: the icon years

ALFRED HITCHCOCK: the icon years

one

ALFRED HITCHCOCK: the icon years

ALFRED HITCHCOCK: the icon years

"There is no terror in the bang, only in the anticipation of it."

Alfred Hitchcock

Introductory Remarks

There have been many excellent books written about Alfred Hitchcock, some of which proved invaluable as reference or research material for the pages that you are about to read. A bibliography of sources is provided in the Appendix of this book detailing the material I used in pulling together my addition to the vast library of works on Alfred Hitchcock.

I would be remiss if I didn't acknowledge those that I find particularly insightful. In particular, Donald Spoto's 1983 biography, *The Dark Side of Genius*, offers one of the most detailed and best written biographies on the life of Alfred Hitchcock and Robert E. Kapsis' 1992 book, *Hitchcock: The Making of a Reputation,* provides a well documented and thoroughly researched analysis of Hitchcock's reputation as an artist and his attempts at shaping his legacy. This book does not aim to accomplish either of those tasks, for they have already been accomplished.

Origins of the Book

Back in the spring of 2000 I was actually asked if I would be interested in doing a biography of Hitchcock. At the time I was trying to sell a publisher on a book idea about another filmmaker, whose career has not been nearly as well chronicled, but they were uninterested in my proposal and passed on the book which was released though another publisher.

Oddly enough however they asked if I would consider doing a book for them on Hitchcock. Having been a fan of Hitchcock's films I always thought it would be interesting to research and write about a man whose career left an indelible mark on cinema. I suggested several ideas I had on projects surrounding Hitchcock's career. One idea was a book on Hitchcock's films from a comedic perspective. Humor was a large component of his work, whether his deadpan dry delivery of his television series monologues or the irony and comedic relief he used throughout his films to cut the tension and suspense, I've long felt it was a territory untouched.

Another idea I had surrounded his relationship and use of "the cool blonde" in his films. It was a central character he carried with him for much of his career and I thought it might make for an interesting tale. Donald Spoto would tackle that idea far better that I ever could a number of years later in his 2008 book *Spellbound by Beauty: Alfred Hitchcock and His Leading Ladies.*

ALFRED HITCHCOCK: the icon years

My suggestions were rejected as the publisher explained that they "wanted a biography of the life of Alfred Hitchcock."

I responded that there had already been so many excellent biographies written about Alfred Hitchcock that I really didn't think I had anything new to contribute to the topic. I ultimately declined the opportunity and don't know if they ever got the book they were looking for from another writer. But I am glad I never tackled such a task. For the world does not need another biography on the master of suspense.

I moved onto other projects, but continued to find myself drawn to the life of Alfred Hitchcock. He would actually find his way into many projects I would work on, including my 2004 book *Reel Horror* and a 2008 book on Irwin Allen entitled *Master of Disaster* as well as my first book *Curse of the Silver Screen* from 1998.

When I had opportunities to meet former leading ladies of Alfred Hitchcock's I jumped at the chance. I actually corresponded with Janet Leigh several times in the 1990s when I was working as a newspaper journalist and she was working on her book *Psycho: Behind the Scenes of the Classic Thriller*. I contacted Miss Leigh while working on an article for a newspaper about *Psycho* and she mentioned she, in fact, was working on a book of her own on the making of the film. And when the book was published in 1995 I was fortunate enough to attend a book signing and meet and speak with her in person. She was very proud of her work in *Psycho* and most grateful for having had the chance to work for Mr. Hitchcock, as she often respectfully referred to him. I found her most insightful and it was a true pleasure meeting her.

Several years later I attended an interview in San Francisco when Tippi Hedren was the center of a tribute to Hitchcock's leading ladies. The event included film clips and a screening of *The Birds*, as well as an interview and question and answer session with Miss Hedren on stage. While I didn't have a chance to meet her personally, I found her insights into working with Hitchcock very helpful. She too was grateful for having had the chance to work for him. While she was reserved about her personal relationship with the man, she suggested that "very few people probably really knew the real Alfred Hitchcock, but rather the persona they saw in his TV appearances or interviews." I suspect she was right.

Tippi Hedren also appeared at a local San Francisco retail tradition, Gumps, to promote a collectible "birds" pin that was a replica of the original one Alfred and Alma gave her when she was offered the role of Melanie Daniels and I had the opportunity to attend the event. She seemed to have come to terms with the ordeal of the making of the film and enjoyed returning to San Francisco, just a few steps from where her opening sequence in *The Birds* was filmed. Her recollections on working with Hitchcock proved invaluable in pulling this book together.

An Idea

So, why a book on Hitchcock now? I suppose it's because I finally found that I did have something to contribute to the story of Alfred Hitchcock. I began thinking about the 50th anniversary of the release of *Psycho* and it occurred to me that the film was truly a turning point in his career. The success of the film raised the bar for him and, in many ways, was the culmination of all his years of hard work discovering what makes a successful and good picture. He proved it did not take lots of money or lots of time.

After the film's release he would find that every work he released thereafter would be considered no more than second best to his 1960 suspense horror feature. And reviewers would begin judging him on his body of work. He would also be crowned the "Master of Suspense" and would find the title one that could be challenging to live up to.

But he would also become an icon. His recognizable face and name would stand for something. I felt that this period was worthy of a look in its own right. For he, in fact, had become a different person. A seasoned filmmaker whose successes afforded him his choice of projects, but it also presented him with a unique set of challenges because he was a brand and a commodity and he stood for thrills, suspense and the macabre. When moviegoers stepped into the theater there was an expectation, sometimes almost too high to live up to. But as filmmaker he was always reaching for new highs and trying to put the film world on notice and on edge.

So, *The Icon Years* is a look at the filmmaker Hitchcock was becoming at the dawn of the 1960s and the struggle he would undergo for the remainder of his life to live up to the title and the expectations placed upon him. Financially his films made him one of the most powerful and successful men in Hollywood and he would spend the rest of his life trying to retain that power and use it wisely. And to create a legacy that would live on for the ages.

The book does not aim to delve into the psyche of Alfred Hitchcock. Several writers have tackled the task of exploring Hitchcock's personality traits and a host of issues, flaws and troubling elements behind the man. We aim in no way to take issue with those reports, but I attempt to steer clear of certain elements to focus more on the work and perception of the filmmaker and the productions of the films themselves. However there is some exploration of certain incidents that impacted the making or release of a film. While Hitchcock, to many, became an icon, he was also a man of faults as well as talents.

- John William Law

ALFRED HITCHCOCK: the icon years

ALFRED HITCHCOCK: the icon years

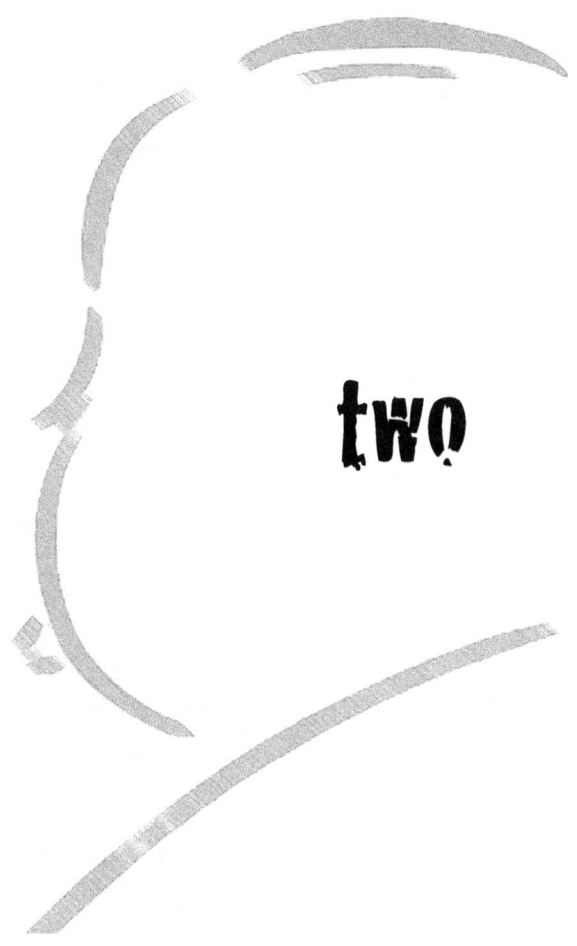

two

ALFRED HITCHCOCK: the icon years

ALFRED HITCHCOCK: the icon years

"Many films are pieces of life. Mine are slices of cake."
Alfred Hitchcock

The Icon & The Man

Reaching for the stars, an icon takes shape

There's no doubt that Alfred Hitchcock is a legend. His brand of filmmaking helped define the suspense genre and his uncanny ability to use himself to promote his films shed new light on the role of the director and he turned, not only himself, but his profession, into a commodity.

Alfred Hitchcock is not known for a single or any number of films, but rather for a body of work that encompassed more than a half-century of filmmaking. From the early 1920s until his final film in 1976 he would capture the imaginations of multiple generations. Even after his passing in 1980 his presence would continue to be felt on the big screen.

When *Psycho II* hit theaters in 1983 it was the opening sequence – Hitchcock's infamous shower scene, featuring the demise of Janet Leigh's Marion Crane that opened up the film and once again caught the attention of moviegoers. His films are still finding new audiences. From re-releases in the theater to packages for DVD, he's everywhere.

Even his TV series is still finding a home on cable television or DVD releases. And book, after book, after book, as well as documentaries, TV specials and magazine articles continue to delve beneath the surface of his life and work. All this from a portly man so full of insecurity that he would rather hide behind a locked door than be forced into a difficult discussion with an actor or writer.

Hitchcock would become as much a performer as a director. It was his deadpan humor and his dry personality, along with his non-confrontational, almost grandfatherly appearance that made him welcoming, even as his subject matter grew gruesome. It was what got him into the living rooms of America for nearly ten years during his television series *Alfred Hitchcock Presents*. Even with the murder and mayhem that pressed all the uncomfortable buttons we had, as well as the network and movie censors, his personality somehow seemed to make it alright or acceptable. Nothing bad could truly come from a man so likeable – could it?

In fact, it was not long after the debut of his TV series *Alfred Hitchcock Presents* than he began on his path toward icon status. He was fast becoming one of the most recognizable faces – or profiles – around the world. He graced TV screens, movie screens, movie posters, advertisements, magazine covers, book covers and billboards every time he released a new film.

And it was after the release of *North by Northwest* that his ascension truly took shape. The film's success showed everyone that he could have it all – a top grossing movie, a hit TV series, a successful series of books and anything else he set his mind to. When *Psycho* hit theaters no one knew what was in store and his icon status took hold. He was now the most successful and well-known director – if not personality – in Hollywood.

An Iconic Figure

An icon, in modern culture, most often embodies a name, face, picture, or a person, recognizable worldwide for its significance within our culture. It carries certain qualities that represent greater significance through some literal or figurative meaning. While usually associated with religious, cultural, political or economic standing, in the world of popular culture some of our most prevalent icons can come from the entertainment industry where they reach millions of people in often overpowering and all-encompassing ways.

For Hitchcock that status really took shape around 1960. After the success of *North by Northwest* and the blockbuster reception of *Psycho* his movie clout couldn't have been greater. And having succeeded in almost every other form of media he was now so well known that stars were no longer an issue for him. He was the star of his motion pictures and everyone else was just an actor or member of the crew. And those who were celebrities took roles in his films without any idea what they'd be acting in. Just the chance to work with Hitchcock was enough. They most often willingly put themselves into his hands so they could be stabbed, pecked, raped or expelled by gas – or whatever else he had in mind.

As for his work, prior to 1960 Hitchcock films were most frequently viewed on their own merit. Most reviews looked at a film for what it delivered – the performance, the direction, cast, sets, location, story, music and other elements helped with the critical success or failure. And reviews would offer each its own opportunity to succeed or fail based upon itself.

But after 1960 and the release of *Psycho* that would seldom be true again. Nearly every feature would be counted and reviewed "among his body of work." *Psycho* itself was originally torn apart by critics who called it "a spectacle of stomach-churning horror." *The New York Times* went so far as to say the film was "a blot on an honorable career." After the film became a smash and broke nearly every box-office record imaginable, reviewers began to re-evaluate the feature and found it to be one of the ten best films of the year by the close of 1960. Hitchcock was even nominated for an Academy Award for Best Director – an honor he would never receive for a feature film.

His films to follow *Psycho* almost always suffered the impossible comparison to what would become his most famous work. But with the success of *Psycho* came re-evaluation of many of his earlier works. Films like *Vertigo, Rear Window, To Catch a Thief, I Confess, Notorious, Rebecca, Strangers on a Train, Lifeboat* and more were given a new look and they became the bedrock of his career. It was with these films that all his future films would be compared. And having covered so many elements of drama, suspense, adventure, thrills, and even comedy his newer films almost always failed to live up to critical expectation. How could they?

But even so, he was still ardently working at his craft. Finding new ways to tell a story and bringing some of Hollywood's heaviest hitters out to help him. And in doing so his auteur status as a filmmaker also took shape. As an icon of celluloid he would find himself being honored with retrospectives of his greatest works at museums and film houses around the world. He was being honored with lifetime achievement awards for his contributions to the world of entertainment and he was being sought after by film aficionados for interviews so they could get inside his head and discover everything he thought about film and anything they could glean from him on what makes a great film or how to record the perfect cinematic sequence.

It was with these awards, interviews and retrospectives that Hitchcock soaked up the adoration and mustered the necessary courage to try again and embark on a new project to recapture his grand past. And it is this period that we discover *Alfred Hitchcock - The Icon Years*.

ALFRED HITCHCOCK: the icon years

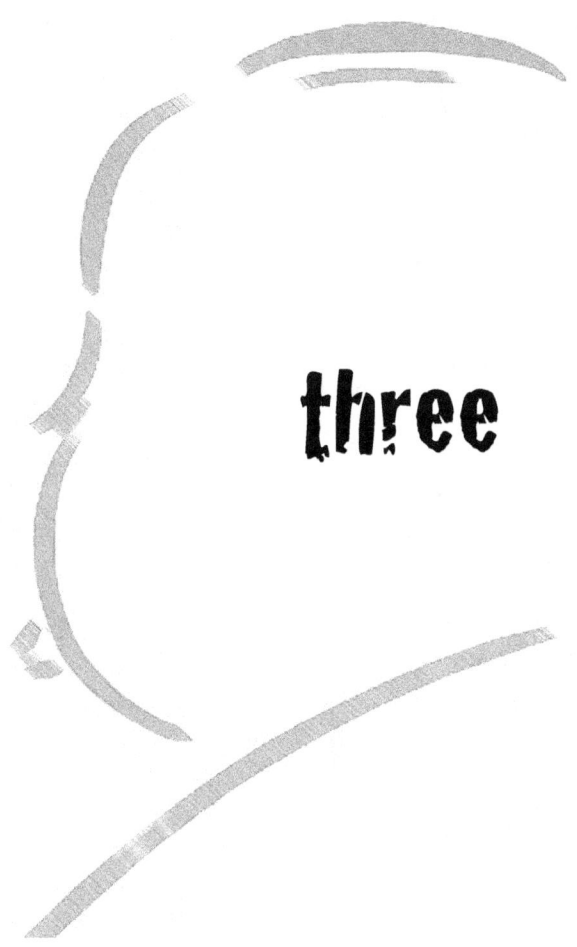

three

ALFRED HITCHCOCK: the icon years

ALFRED HITCHCOCK: the icon years

"One must never set up a murder. They must happen unexpectedly, as in life."

Alfred Hitchcock

The Early Years

From London to Hollywood, a career in motion

Alfred Hitchcock was born August 13, 1899 in Leytonstone, London. He was the second and youngest son of William and Emma Jane Hitchcock. He also had a sister. His childhood has been described as both lonely and sheltered. And heavyset from the time he was very young, it was a condition that would plague him his entire life and only compounded his situation, making him increasingly shy and more reclusive. He claimed that as a young boy he was sent by his father to the local police station with a note asking the officer to lock him in a cell as punishment for bad behavior.

While it was only a short span of about five or ten minutes Hitchcock was heavily influenced by the incident and harbored a lifelong fear of policemen and incarceration and he would include many such events in his films. His father would die when he was 14 and that event as well would also have an impact on the characters and stories of his future projects.

After graduating from school, he became a draftsman and advertising designer, but his interest in photography lead him to work with a film production company in London.

He obtained a full-time job at Islington Studios designing movie titles for silent films in 1920. Over the next several years he would explore numerous other avenues in the film business until 1925 when he began directing silent movies.

In December 1926 he married his assistant director, Alma Reville and their only child, a daughter named Patricia, was born in July 1928. By the 1930s, with experience, his talents improved and by the end of the decade he was one of the most successful filmmakers in the United Kingdom. Soon Hollywood came calling.

Coming to Hollywood

In 1939 David O. Selznick signed Hitchcock to a seven-year contract and the director relocated to Los Angeles with his family and began what would be a very prolific but at times difficult period for Hitchcock. While thrilled to be able to make big-budget motion pictures that masses of moviegoers could enjoy, Hitchcock was often frustrated by Selznick's struggle for creative control over his films. But out of the struggle for power Hitchcock would create a some of his most memorable and challenging films. It was during this period that he, with the help of Selznick would direct the Oscar-winning *Rebecca* in 1940. While the film earned the Academy Award for Best Picture of 1940 for Selznick, Hitchcock was denied the Best Director award. But he would go on to direct numerous other notable classics of the decade including *Suspicion* (1941), *Saboteur* (1942), *Shadow of a Doubt* (1943), *Lifeboat* (1944) and *Notorious* (1946).

He also had some notable failures during this time that prevented him from being viewed as Hollywood's golden boy. Lackluster response to films like *The Paradine Case* (1947) and *Under Capricorn* (1949) would frustrate Hitchcock and he would blame others for preventing him from achieving his goal. He would later seek out opportunities to produce his own films in his later years in order to retain as much creative control as possible.

With the 1950s he would produce many of his most recognizable work, including *Strangers on a Train* (1951), *Rear Window* (1954), *Dial M for Murder* (1954), *Vertigo* (1958) and *North by Northwest* (1959). But like the 1940s he would have several missteps with disappointing releases in *Stage Fright* (1950) and *The Wrong Man* (1957).

The Small Screen Too

Hitch would also move into the world of television with his TV series *Alfred Hitchcock Presents* in 1955 and lend his name to a successful series of paperback books that carried the trademark tales of suspense and macabre that would make his television show a success with viewers for a decade.

And with roughly 30 years of film experience his name would draw attention to the relatively new medium of television drama. And once it did, his face became better known than many of his actors. Although he only directed 17 half-hour or hour-long episodes of his show, the series would air some 350 episodes, and like his books, he would be putting his face on every episode, almost stamping the work of others as his own. It was his style and his show. And one of the trademarks of the series was the iconic Hitchcock silhouette, which reportedly came from a sketch used for a Christmas card designed by Hitchcock.

The show would do quite well in the ratings during its first few seasons, moving between fourth and sixth place, behind staples like *The Ed Sullivan Show* and *Lucy*. In its second season it would earn an Emmy Award for writing. The series would also prove financially rewarding. Hitchcock's contract would earn him $129,000 per show, as well as all rights of sale and rebroadcast after each show first aired. For production he set up a television company, Shamley Productions, named after a summer home he and his wife purchased in Shamley Green, a small village south of London, back in 1928. Hitch's contract with his sponsor Bristol-Meyers stipulated that he would only direct an "unspecified number of episodes" each season, allowing him to continue to focus on his feature films.

His TV series aired on CBS from 1955 until 1960 when it was picked up by NBC in 1960. After two seasons on NBC, CBS brought the show back to its network, but this time as an hour-long show and renaming it *The Alfred Hitchcock Hour*. Its final season, in 1964, would be on NBC, also in an hour-long format.

Hitch would also directed two other noteworthy television shows during this period. One was an episode of a drama called *Suspicion* in 1957 and the other was an episode of *Ford Star Time* in 1960. His television work allowed him to work with a planned schedule, something his film actors would grow accustomed to on is later films. He ended his day at 4 p.m. and enjoyed the regularity of a schedule. His half-hour dramas were filmed in three days and the hour-long shows in five. And even though he didn't direct the bulk of the shows his mark was left on each. He selected each show that would be filmed and oversaw many of the key production decisions. He would even employ many members of his TV crew on future film work and a number of the actors in his shows would find their way into his films.

But it was his personality, his name and his face on the movie screen, the TV screen and in bookstores, presenting the Hitchcock brand of macabre suspense. And this would help make him an icon. He would put the director's role on the map and turn himself into a television and movie star. His image would be recognizable across the globe and he would be one of the most popular and successful personalities in Hollywood.

ALFRED HITCHCOCK: the icon years

ALFRED HITCHCOCK: the icon years

four

ALFRED HITCHCOCK: the icon years

ALFRED HITCHCOCK: the icon years

"After all, I'm sure you will agree that murder can be so much more charming and enjoyable even for the victim, if the surroundings are pleasant and the people involved are ladies and gentlemen like yourselves."

Alfred Hitchcock

Closing out the 50s

A major hit in theaters, Hitchcock closes out the decade on a high note as icon status waits

When Alfred Hitchcock completed *North by Northwest* in the spring of 1959 he had been on the climb to top of his craft. The film, released that summer would take the director out of the 1950s on a high note and mark his ascension to the status of an icon. It would be a huge box office hit, earning a reported $13.2 million.

The 50s had been a mixture of success and failure, of high hopes and dashed expectations for Alfred Hitchcock. Some of his most critically acclaimed work would help mark his ascension, while his lackluster releases would hinder it and prove he wasn't quite as unshakable as he tried to convince studio heads and the public of. With *Vertigo* and *Rear Window* he would break new ground and offer moviegoers something unexpected.

His vast experience behind the camera had given him new insight into marrying the image, the action, the spoken word, music and location in a way that offered so many layers of storytelling that it would take years of viewing the films to fully understand their meaning and offer decades of enjoyment to film aficionados. The films would even find release and re-release for years, as new viewers would discover the films for the first time while longtime fans would rediscover a classic.

With Hits Come Misses

But if his successes put him on the verge of greatness, his failures would humble him – not in a public way, but in the privacy of his own offices, his home and his mind. They would keep him insecure and craving public acceptance. He claimed he never got angry, but those who knew him well would argue that wasn't quite true.

While he was prone to occasional angry outbursts, they were few and far between. But when they happened everyone knew about them. In most instances it was his silence that dealt the deathblow. He would become sullen or silent and in an instant turn from friend into foe. He would ignore people for days, weeks or years. He would punish people with his silence and never truly acknowledge or publicly discuss the reasons behind his anger. He would often leave the dirty work to others and suddenly a writer, actor or fellow filmmaker would find him or herself out in the cold. Many have spoken of such treatment.

With lackluster receptions of films like *Under Capricorn* in 1949, *Stage Fright* in 1950, *I Confess* in 1952, and *The Trouble with Harry* in 1956, he was left with the feeling he always had something more to prove. And in many ways he did.

With *North by Northwest* he had achieved something great. It was both a critical and box office success. It offered everything that Hitchcock did best in combining suspense with humor, romance and adventure. With a cast that included his quintessential leading man, Cary Grant, and a supporting cast of amazing actors like Eva Marie Saint, James Mason, Martin Landau, and Jessie Royce Landis, the film succeeded on every level.

Then There Was TV

As the decade came to a close he was not only a name on the marquee, but he was a face in America's living rooms with his weekly TV series *Alfred Hitchcock Presents*. The show debuted in the fall season of 1955 and would quickly grow on TV viewers. It was a top rated series by the end of the decade. As the 60s came into view his show was going as strong as ever.

While he didn't direct most of the episodes his story selections and his introductions of them made him one of the most recognizable faces in Hollywood – often more so than many of his stars. And he branded the tales his, even though they were most often directed by others and he had little involvement in their actual production.

His deadpan and often droll delivery of his introductory messages often went something like this:

> "Good evening, ladies and gentlemen, and welcome to darkest Hollywood. Night brings stillness to the jungle. It is so quiet, you can hear a name drop. The savage

beasts have already begun gathering at the water holes to quench their thirst. Now one should be especially alert. The vicious table-hopper is on the prowl, and the spotted back-biter may lurk behind a potted palm."

A Successful Brand

And if that wasn't enough he lent his name and face to other products as well. He offered a magazine for fans and even a board game. But of most note, there was a successful series of paperback books from Dell Publishing. Collections of short stories, written by others, that again carried his brand of suspense coupled with twists and turns, were pocketbook favorites that kept him front and center in bookstores and markets everywhere. Along with his series, they also helped make him a very wealthy man even if his big screen features didn't always make a big profit.

His books included titles like *12 Stories They Wouldn't Let Me Do on TV*, *14 of My Favorites in Suspense*, *Bar the Doors*, *More Stories Late at Night*, and *More of My Favorites in Suspense*.

He even introduced the books with the same banter of his TV show. "Murder is a fine art and needs the embellishment of a sophisticated imagination," he wrote in one introduction. "The true aficionado prefers to have his nerves ruffled by the implied threats – the Bourgeois rather than the syndicate. What is more delightful than a domestic crime, when it is executed with subtlety and imagination? I leave to other more pedestrian talents materials based on newspaper accounts. True crimes, ugh! Alas, most of them are dull and give no evidence of the careful planning and loving thought that should go into any human activity as rewarding as murder."

It was ironic in retrospect, considering that the film he would release in 1960, his follow-up to *North by Northwest*, would in fact be taken from the headlines and based on a real-life murder case, But we're getting ahead of ourselves.

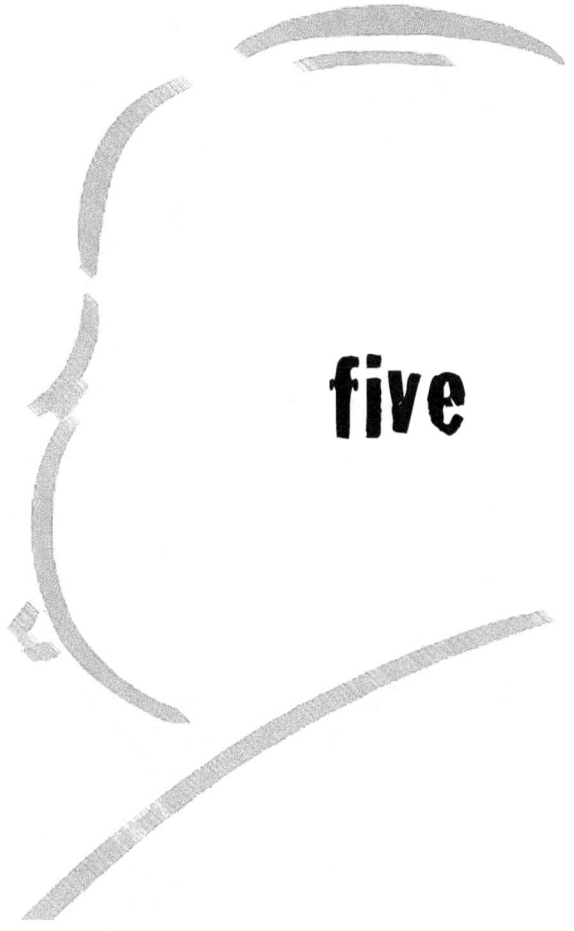

five

ALFRED HITCHCOCK: the icon years

ALFRED HITCHCOCK: the icon years

"Nothing is more revolting than the underworld thug who is able to murder anyone — even people to who he has not been properly introduced."

Alfred Hitchcock

No Bail for the Judge

Unfinished film leaves the director searching for something new

In April 1959 Alfred Hitchcock boarded a flight for his homeland. Returning to the United Kingdom and familiar London haunts, Hitchcock was in the pre-planning phase of his next film. Like London itself, the film would travel familiar ground for the world famous director, but it would also be a departure of sorts. The film was *No Bail for the Judge*. For starters, it would be a noted departure because its star was not a cool beautiful blonde. Yes, the star would be beautiful and cool, but she was the farthest thing from blonde. She was Audrey Hepburn.

Audrey Hepburn was, in many ways, perfect for a Hitchcock film. While not blonde, her beauty was tempered with an innate comedic ability, as well as an aloofness and coolness that somehow created a charm that made her intensely likeable in even the most awkward of characters. From her early starring roles in *Sabrina* and *Roman Holiday* she commanded attention, sometimes at the expense of her leading male counterparts like Humphrey Bogart, William Holden and Gregory Peck.

In the summer of 1959, just as pre-planning for *No Bail for the Judge* would move into high gear she was at the top of her game again in what some have called one of her finest performance, an Oscar-nominated role as Sister Luke in *A Nun's Story*. She would also win a BAFTA film award as Best British Actress for the role.

Hepburn was actually filming another movie, *The Unforgiven* for John Huston and she was injured when she was thrown from a horse during a scene in Mexico. She was pregnant at the time and the event caused a scare as the actress and her husband very much wanted children. Neither she or her husband wanted her to go into any risky situations that might harm her unborn child. After a stay in the hospital, Hepburn was at home recuperating when she received a treatment for Hitchcock's film.

The Cool Brunette

Now, Hepburn initially agreed to star in the Hitchcock film for several obvious reasons. For starters, nearly any actor in Hollywood would agree to star in a Hitchcock film without ever having to look at a script. The famed director was often sought after and most actors longed for a chance to be directed by the most famous director of the time and would sign on, sight-unseen, to anything being planned by him.

ALFRED HITCHCOCK: the icon years

In addition, Hitchcock was every bit a women's director and his films offered great challenges for any actress. His female characters often held central roles that were as vital to the story as the male characters in his films. He also lavished great attention on his female leads when it came to costumes, make-up, hair and lighting and every actress knew she would come off looking her best in front of a Hitchcock camera.

One change the director did want to make was not surprising - he wanted her blonde. Hitchcock hoped to have Audrey dye her hair for the picture so she would continue his theme of golden-haired leading ladies. Hepburn initially told the director she was "looking forward to reading he script" and she would "do anything he wanted" based on the story he had told her.

London Preparations

By the time Hitch landed in London he was ready for the prep work that was about it begin. He planned to scout the perfect shooting locations for his feature as well and focus attention on some of the legal aspects of the British court system for some key story elements. To launch his films of the 1960s he need suspense, adventure and romance, but he also needed it to be factual. He certainly wanted to keep in the frame of his most recent work, *North by Northwest*. Even though the film was not yet in theaters, it was turning into something special and many knew it.

Herbert Coleman, Henry Bumstead and Samuel Taylor, accompanied Hitchcock on the trip to assist with the research and location scouting. Hitchcock was reportedly agitated at the circus-like atmosphere in Los Angeles International Airport as the wives and children of his traveling companions attended the send-off. But as the trip took shape he was quite excited by the potential the film held. Hitchcock always enjoyed the preparation, scripting nuances and planning the shots of his films far more than the actual shooting. He often claimed that by the time the filming was taking place he had already worked out the entire feature in his head and was no longer interested in the camera work, but only in supervising that the camera to capture the scene he had worked out in advance.

One of the many key components of the feature that he had already worked out was the cast of co-stars who would perform alongside Miss Hepburn. John Williams was cast as the central role of the judge, while Laurence Harvey would carry the important role of Hepburn's romantic lead as a handsome thief, not unlike Cary Grant's role in *To Catch a Thief*.

John Williams was very much a part of Hitchcock's inner circle of familiar faces, having worked with the director many times. Not only had he starred in 10 episodes of *Alfred Hitchcock Presents*, including *Banco's Chair*, the most recent May 1959 episode directed by Hitchcock himself, but Williams also worked with the director on several of his most notable feature films including *The Paradine Case* in 1947, *Dial M For Murder* in 1954 and *To Catch a Thief* in 1955. He also worked with Audrey Hepburn in *Sabrina* in 1954.

Laurence Harvey, on the other hand was relatively new to working with the likes of Alfred Hitchcock. Harvey had started out in a series of small roles in forgettable films in the late 1940s but would work steadily through the 50s, never really hitting his stride until *Room at the Top* in 1959 and *Butterfield 8* in 1960. He would also go onto further fame in 1962 opposite Frank Sinatra in the classic *The Manchurian Candidate*. He never worked for Hitchcock before but after his feature film role fell through he would fulfill his contractual agreement for the director by performing in an episode of *Alfred Hitchcock Presents* in 1959 called *Arthur*. He was a handsome, brooding actor, traits that would suit his character well in *No Bail for the Judge*.

The three lead actors were all initially given a brief treatment of the film with a synopsis of the story and all agreed it sounded like a wonderful feature for Hitchcock and wanted very much to take part in.

ALFRED HITCHCOCK: the icon years

Based on a novel of the same name by Henry Cecil, *No Bail for the Judge* centered on a mysterious tale of a capital cases judge in London's Old Bailey Court. The author was actually Henry Cecil Leon, an actual British justice who slightly altered his name for the pen name of the novel. The role of the judge was intended for John Williams.

While walking home one evening the judge falls and hits his head on the pavement after he dodges into the street to save a dog that is nearly run down by a London taxi. He gets up and staggers away from the scene a bit confused and is taken in by a prostitute who crosses his path and thinks he is simply a drunk.

The next morning the judge awakens to discover the prostitute's corpse atop him with a knife protruding from her back. Thinking as a judge and aiming to do the right thing, he calls the police, but claims he doesn't recall much of the evening. Unsure whether he is guilty of murder, the judge is taken to prison to await trial. His daughter, the role intended for Hepburn, is that of a lawyer who believes her father innocent and sets out to prove it. She heads to her father's home and catches a handsome young thief, Harvey's intended role, but instead of turning him into the police, she agrees to let him go on the grounds that he helps her infiltrate London's prostitution underworld in hopes of solving the crime and finding out who the real murderer is. The couple head off on a dark mission to uncover the truth and some sparks between the two are never far from possibility.

A Paramount Release

To be produced by Paramount Studios, the filming was set to take place in London and be shot in Technicolor and VistaVision. It would herald in the 60s as Hitchcock's latest masterpiece along the lines of *Vertigo*, a film that offered a lush and colorful, but dark tale set in San Francisco several years earlier. Unlike his black and white films with moody atmosphere, the color film would capture London, as well as

Hepburn and Harvey at their best. Contracts were drawn up and casting of Hitchcock's next picture was announced. But then Audrey Hepburn lost her baby. She headed off to Switzerland to recuperate but initially still intended to film Hitchcock's picture, so plans continued.

One of the challenges Hitchcock faced was in updating the story slightly due to changes in the legal system in Britain in its treatment of prostitution. Ernest Lehman was originally tasked with the job of writing the screenplay for the film but eventually removed himself from the picture because he had misgivings about the story. Samuel Taylor took over the writing responsibilities and focused on making the story more plausible.

The feature also needed enough action and suspense peppered throughout the story to keeping moviegoers focused on the mystery at hand. Hitchcock was not as interested in they mystery, but rather in the suspense, the action and a leading lady in peril.

Hitchcock arranged for Taylor to spend some time getting the realities of the story first hand by talking to a prostitute who had changed careers and was now working as a London secretary. Meeting at the Paramount offices in London, Taylor got an earful about masochism and the lively London sex trade. He was then required to recount all the tales verbatim for Hitchcock who was captivated by the lurid sexuality of it all.

In one of the climactic sequences intended to capture some of the darker underbelly of world of prostitution and the dramatic story behind the film Taylor included a scene where the leading lady is dragged into London's Hyde Park and raped – or nearly raped, that is, by her assailant.

By late May, Hitchcock and his traveling companions returned to Los Angeles with the major elements worked out. The entire tale was committed to paper, with nearly every scene and line of dialogue worked out. A final script soon was completed and ready for the actors shortly after their return.

As *The Nun's Story* was doing big box office and acclaim for its star was rolling in, Audrey Hepburn received the script for her next picture and cringed at the idea of being raped on film for all the world to see. Even though the scene was to be done discretely and with little emotional anguish to the star, Hepburn was reluctant to expose herself to such a scene. In fact she and her husband had been planning to try again for a child and the actress had no intention of putting herself or a child she expected to be carrying in danger by being dragged around a movie set or the real Hyde Park. Hepburn would in fact find out she was pregnant in the fall of 1958 and had she agreed to do the film would have had to endure the terrible treatment Hitchcock had planned for her.

Audrey Hepburn declined to appear in *No Bail for the Judge* and Hitchcock hit the roof. He was beside himself with anger. He had already spent approximately $200,000 on preparing for the film and to lose his star caused him great discomfort. In fact, at this stage he actually lost all interest in the film and told Paramount it would be better for them to cut their losses now rather than invest another $3 million in a film he no longer wanted to make.

And to add insult to injury Hitchcock's *North by Northwest* had to delay its release because *The Nun's Story* was being extended at movie houses across the United States. And then to top it off he lost first prize awards at both The San Sebastian International Film Festival and The Venice Film Festival to *The Nun's Story*.

He would never forgive Audrey Hepburn for walking away from him. Some say he as much as "hated her" after that disappointment. He had grown very frustrated with female stars who abandon him for husbands and children. Grace Kelly and Vera Miles had both caused him great anguish by allowing marriage or pregnancy to get in the way of his work and Audrey Hepburn didn't help matters. Hepburn would go on to film a very successful Hitchcockian feature several years later, with Cary Grant no less. The film was *Charade*. And Hepburn would work with Hitch, sort of in 1966 when she filmed a scene in *How to Steal a Million* reading an Alfred Hitchcock paperback. But what really troubled Hitchcock was what would he deliver to Paramount for his next film.

ALFRED HITCHCOCK: the icon years

ALFRED HITCHCOCK: the icon years

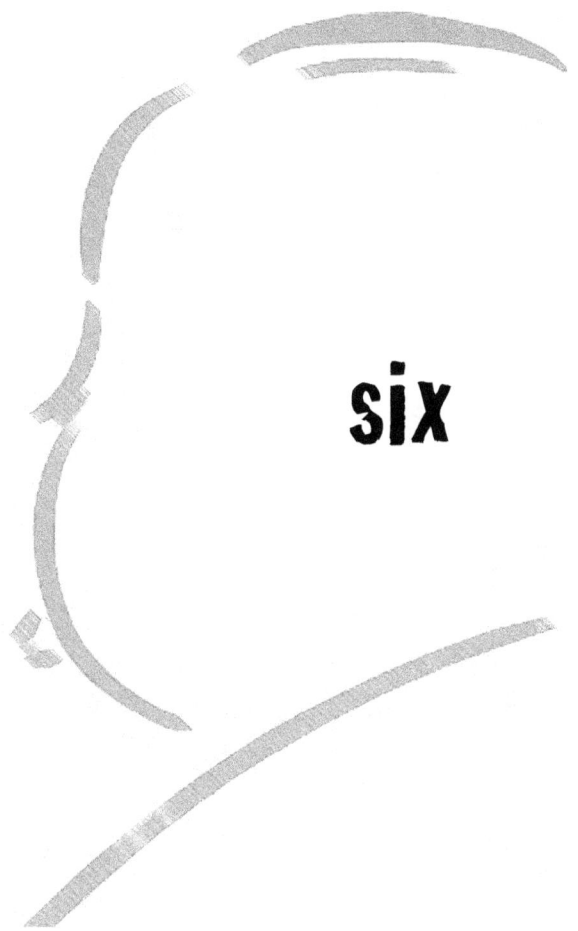

ALFRED HITCHCOCK: the icon years

ALFRED HITCHCOCK: the icon years

"Some of our most exquisite murders have been domestic; performed with tenderness in simple, homey places like the kitchen or the bathtub."

Alfred Hitchcock

Psycho

Murder in the heartland mirrored on the big screen in horrific Hitchcock suspense classic

After the success of *North by Northwest* Hitchcock was already looking for suitable options for his next film. While *No Bail for the Judge* with Audrey Hepburn was the one that got the lion's share of the director's attention, another film was in the running as well. *The Wreck of the Mary Deare* was another production that came forth as Hitchcock was in the throws of *North by Northwest*. It was based on a novel by Hammond Innes that tells the story of the captain of a small rescue ship in the English Channel, who finds a freighter called the Mary Deare adrift at sea. The crew seems to have vanished so as the finder, the captain, thinks he is in line for a large salvage fee. However, before he can take his salvage rights, he discovers the first officer still on board and the officer sends him away. Thus begins a mystery about what happened aboard the Mary Deare as an investigation of the incident follows.

The novel was optioned by MGM and the plan was to have Alfred Hitchcock direct the film and Gary Cooper star. Hitchcock reportedly wanted to work with Cooper, and Hitch was initially interested in the idea. With the help of writer Ernest Lehman, Hitch tried for weeks to craft an interesting story out of the tale. While the film had elements of both drama and mystery, Hitchcock's trademark suspense was in short supply. Eventually, the director concluded a movie version of the book would be nothing more than "a boring courtroom drama," so he abandoned the idea.

The Wreck of the Mary Deare, however, would find its way to the big screen after all when MGM hired writer Eric Ambler to produce the screenplay and Michael Anderson to direct Gary Cooper and Charlton Heston in the feature. The film would hit theaters at the very end of 1959, just as Hitchcock was filming *Psycho*. But Hitchcock was right and the film would never achieve the success of *North By Northwest* or *Psycho*.

Macabre in Middle America

In the fall of 1955 Alfred Hitchcock stepped off the big screen and into America's living rooms with the launch of his television series, *Alfred Hitchcock Presents*. From 1955 until the early 1960s Hitchcock delivered some 350 episodes that carried his trademark stories of suspense, dark humor and macabre, but in television features that were substantially less expensive than his traditional big screen features. While Hitchcock only directed a handful of the shows he was instrumental in their selection and appeared in snippets during each show to deliver his own view on the macabre and how it can come in the most unusual places and take many forms. It delighted his fans and made him one of the most familiar faces in Hollywood.

Two years after Hitchcock took to the airwaves, in 1957, the macabre took America's heartland by surprise when horrifically real images of horror no longer filled viewers' TV screens, but they found their way into the backyard. Hitchcock himself probably wasn't surprised, that's what he believed all along and was exactly why his films and TV shows were popular all over the world.

It was winter in Wisconsin when police received a report that 58-year-old Bernice Worden was missing. After locating her pick-up truck, police were led to a nearby farmhouse owned by Edward Gein where they found Worden's body in a shed. She had been shot and her body was reportedly cut open. She was missing her head, and her corpse was left hanging by its heels. Her heart was cut out and left in a coffee can on the stove. In addition, police soon discovered body parts of 15 other women. Masks of skin, preserved body parts, strips of skin used to cover chairs, and a bowl carved out of a skull, were just some of the atrocities police uncovered.

Gein was located and arrested a short time later without incident. Neighbors were shocked that this quiet man, who was long considered harmless, could be guilty of such horrors. Neighbor Georgia Foster reportedly heard about the story on the news and recalled talking about it with a neighbor. "Neither one of us could believe that he would hurt anybody. We just knew Eddie wouldn't hurt a fly," she said. "So I went home and locked my door for the first time in years."

In 1958, Ed Gein was found not guilty by reason of insanity and was committed to a mental hospital. At about the same time, author Robert Bloch was crafting a fictional story based on the horrors he had heard about in Wisconsin. He didn't chronicle the specifics of the case, but his fictional characterizations came somewhat close to the real Gein house of horrors and it provided him with many of the ideas he would develop his macabre tale from. *Psycho* was the novel he created.

From Novel to Film

Alfred Hitchcock came across the novel and suspected it might make and interesting film. His agents at MCA approached author Robert Bloch, offering him $5,000 for the film rights. The agents never said it was Hitchcock who was interested in the project for fear that the writer would want more money. Even so, Bloch turned the offer down, knowing he could get more. He was right, and a few days later the agents returned with an offer of $9,500. Bloch accepted. "My agent got ten percent, my publishers took fifteen, the tax people skimmed off their share of the loot, and I ended up with about $6,250. Hitchcock got *Psycho*, and the rest is history," Bloch once said.

Currently working at Paramount, Hitchcock approached key executives about producing the film for the studio, but Paramount felt the story was a bit tawdry and didn't like the idea of Alfred Hitchcock's plans for filming a black and white horror picture. The studio lost money the last time they gave the go ahead on a production that strayed from his standard format — *The Trouble With Harry* in 1956 and shouldered the bill from his last unfinished project, *No Bail for the Judge,* and turned the director down.

Not one to give up, Hitchcock decided he could go it alone and would utilize the production services of his television series crew, Shamley Productions, to fund the film himself. Imitators had long been copying the Hitchcock style with low budget, black and white productions that drew in crowds of teenagers. William Castle, in fact had and would continue to make such a name for himself, down to even imitating Hitchcock's TV show logo and his macabre but humorous introductions to this films.

Hitchcock felt he could outdo imitators like Castle and produce his own low-budget thriller. To accomplish this, he filmed the picture on the

Universal lots where his television series was being made and decided to stay away from expensive Hollywood stars to carry the picture. He also kept the time schedule in line with a TV show to streamline the shoot.

Hitchcock was reportedly told that Bloch was unavailable to write the screenplay, even though some say this was simply not true. Even so, the director chose a young writer named Joseph Stephano to craft the screenplay.

For casting, the only major star, besides Hitchcock himself, attached to the project, was Janet Leigh. Leigh had carried a number of pictures and found great success in Hollywood in films like *Little Women, The Naked Spur, Scaramouche* and *Houdini* and her marriage to Tony Curtis made her quite popular with both the press and the public. Hitchcock felt she would be perfect in the role of Marion Crane because people wouldn't expect the only major star of the picture to die so early into the film. Leigh was apparently the only actress offered the role. She accepted in October, 1959. She once remarked she would have done almost anything just for the "opportunity to work with Mr. Hitchcock."

Leigh recalled that Hitchcock, as usual, was more concerned about the image he captured than her acting. "I'm not going to tell you how to act," she said he told her. "If I didn't think you could act I wouldn't have you in my picture. I'm telling you the qualities I need, where I need certain points, and I'll remind you as we do the scenes what the sequence is, and then you can do whatever you like. If you're not up I'll tell you. If you're too up, I'll tell you. But as long as your concept of her [Marion Crane] doesn't interfere with what I need from her, do whatever you want."

Anthony Perkins was well known throughout Hollywood, but had not reached star status by the time *Psycho* was made. He received an Oscar nomination for *Friendly Persuasion* and was co-starring in Stanley Kramer's *On The Beach* when the role came up. He was also reportedly eager to work with Hitchcock. Vera Miles, who had starred in *The Wrong Man* and was under contract was cast in the role of Marion's sister Lila, and John

Gavin took on the part of Marion's boyfriend, Sam Loomis. Martin Balsam was also brought on board as a nosey police detective. The cast was one of competent actors, but none too expensive or too glamorous to overshadow the darkness of the picture.

Shot much like his television series, the film was quite inexpensive by Hollywood standards, costing approximately $860,000 to make. Filming began in late November and ended around early January. The film's most famous scene, the shower scene murder of Marion Crane, took place two days before Christmas, 1959. Storyboards by art director Saul Bass detailed the scene and Hitchcock shot it over about a week and included between 70 and 80 shots for the brief scene. Actor Anthony Perkins wasn't even around when the famous murder scene was shot. He was actually in New York rehearsing for a play and his stand-in was used for the sequence. Dark make-up was used to shield his face even more than normal to keep the illusion that mother is up to no good.

The film was shot on a restricted set and little was released about the picture, causing Hollywood to wonder about Hitch's mysterious new project. Even the clapper for the production was altered to throw people off track. The name "Wimpy" was used early on and few knew Hitchcock had purchased the rights to *Psycho* because he didn't want to give the secrets of the story away by reading the book first.

For the role of mother, Janet Leigh recalled that several dummy corpses were created. She has said that to test them out Hitchcock would leave them sitting in her dressing room and her screams were usually the approval he was looking for. She supposed that the loudest scream resulted in the corpse used in the picture.

The Big Release

The film was edited, the infamous score added, and a marketing campaign that said no one would be admitted to the film after it began was developed and finally the film was released in June 1960.

ALFRED HITCHCOCK: the icon years

No one knew what to expect.

Hitchcock handled most of the promotion himself, not using Perkins or Leigh for fear some of the film's secrets would get out. He filmed a trailer that was actually a tour of the Bates house and motel and in the end when a shower curtain is pulled open the screaming woman was Vera Miles, not Janet Leigh. Hitchcock wanted to hide the facts and keep the public guessing.

It premiered on June 16, 1960. The film was an astounding success. It reportedly broke all box-office records in the Canada, China, France, Great Britain, Japan and the United States and pulled in $9.1 million in its first release. Later reports have earnings surpassing $16 million through its initial run.

Subsequent releases continued bring in money as the film would be re-released in theaters numerous times. Ultimately its success would make it the director's most financially successful picture ever with estimates of it earning as much at $32 million in theatrical release alone. Patrons lined up around the block to see what all the fuss was about and everyone was talking about the movie.

But the reviewers were initially not so kind to the picture. Perhaps it was because Hitchcock had gone out of his way to keep them in the dark. Not wanting to give away the picture's secrets, some had difficulty making screening early enough to write reviews for their daily newspapers. In some cases, early press screenings were held at times that made it nearly impossible for reviewers to meet their deadlines, in effect, keeping the writers from telling the public about the film before its release.

Time magazine wrote, "Director Hitchcock bears down too heavily in this one, and the delicate illusion of reality necessary for a creak-and shriek movie becomes, instead, a spectacle of stomach-churning horror."

The *New York Times* called it "a blot on an honorable career," and *Esquire* said it was "... merely one of those television shows padded out to two hours by adding pointless subplots and realistic detail ..."

But in the end it was the public that rated the picture number one and eventually the reviewers began to come around. By the end of the year many critics had reevaluated the film and selected it as one of the ten best of the year. One reviewer even said it was "the most astounding, audacious and successful horror film ever made."

After-Effects

Psycho was a huge success and set the stage for magnificent things to come. Hitchcock was nominated for an Academy Award for best director and Janet Leigh was nominated for an Oscar for her performance. It was up for Best Cinematography and Art Direction. It did not win an award, although Leigh was honored with a Golden Globe award for her part in the film. Anthony Perkins was not nominated. Hitchcock however also received a nomination as best director from the Directors Guild of America for his work.

In the years that followed, *Psycho* placed its key players in a lofty position in which many of them found it difficult to survive professionally. Hitchcock himself ended his TV series as viewers began to lose interest. His film work continued, but it was hard to top *Psycho*. His next effort, *The Birds* continued his work in the genre of horror, but again received little praise from the critics. The film initially did well at the box office, but never captured the imagination of the public the way *Psycho* did. Most of his later features did not meet expectations at the box office and with the reviewers, until the mid-1970 when *Frenzy* and *Family Plot* gave him some renewed success, but not nearly at the level of *Psycho*.

Both Anthony Perkins and Janet Leigh struggled to overcome their success in the film. Leigh managed best with films like *Bye Bye Birdie* and *The Manchurian Candidate*, but as the decade wore on the roles grew fewer. In the early 1970s she starred in another horror film, *Night of the Lepus,* which was panned by the critics and by moviegoers. And frighteningly enough, she was plagued by death threats after *Psycho*'s release. For years she claimed she would get horrible letters that she turned over to the authorities. Fortunately, nothing ever came of the threats.

Leigh continued to work in Hollywood successfully, including several notable horror roles that harkened back to her time with Hitchcock. John Carpenter cast her in a central role in his hit film, *The Fog*, in 1980 and she would play opposite her daughter, Jamie Lee Curtis, in both *The Fog* and in one of her final roles *Halloween H20: 20 years Later* in 2000. Leigh died in 2004.

For Anthony Perkins the role of Norman Bates cast a shadow over his career. Most of the roles offered him were of the same character and Perkins resisted as best he could, but work was somewhat difficult to come by on the big screen.

Finally, in the early 80s Perkins returned to the role that made him famous and capitalized on the success, filming several sequels in the *Psycho* series and directing one himself. But even still, he never escaped the original. In fact, in part because he resisted being typecast as Norman Bates he didn't work as often as he might have. And by the time he accepted his fate and returned to the role it was nearly too late to do much else.

Anthony Perkins died in 1992. His final performance was in a TV horror/mystery called *In the Deep Woods* that capitalized on his notoriety as Norman Bates.

One interesting note to the story behind *Psycho* is that the Gein case was the subject of another series of films as well. *The Texas Chainsaw Massacre* horror films are also reportedly based on the story of Ed Gein, however, while the films earned significant box office dollars and enjoy a cult following, they never achieved the success *Psycho* did.

For Hitchcock his foray into horror had turned him into one of the most profitable and successful commodities in Hollywood. And it would not be his last. In fact, his most technically challenging film was already forming in his mind's eye. And film historians have noted that many references to his next film would turn up in *Psycho*.

A Suspenseful Next Picture

For the director, following up *Psycho* would be a daunting task. Initially Hitchcock set his sights on a film called *The Blind Man*. He once again sought out the talents of Ernest Lehman for what would be an original screenplay.

The tale is that of a blind pianist named Jimmy Shearing, a role Hitchcock intended on having James Stewart play. Hitch and Stewart had worked together many times and were very comfortable with each other.

The story takes off when the blind man regains his sight after receiving the eyes of a dead man. With his new sight, the man takes his family to Disneyland and during a Wild West gun battle he begins to have visions of being shot at. At first he doesn't understand what's happening to him, but he soon comes to discover that the eyes he received were from a dead man who was murdered. Suspense comes when he realizes the image of the murderer is still imprinted on the retina of his new eyes.

A cat-and-mouse-like climax of the film was expected to take place aboard the ocean liner, RMS Queen Mary. And things seemed as if they were off to a good start until Walt Disney reportedly refused to allow Hitchcock to shoot at Disneyland. After seeing *Psycho*, Disney didn't seem to think that films from the master of suspense were suitable for the whole family. When details couldn't be ironed out James Stewart eventually left the project in favor of another and Hitchcock lost interest and moved on. The film would never be shot.

ALFRED HITCHCOCK: the icon years

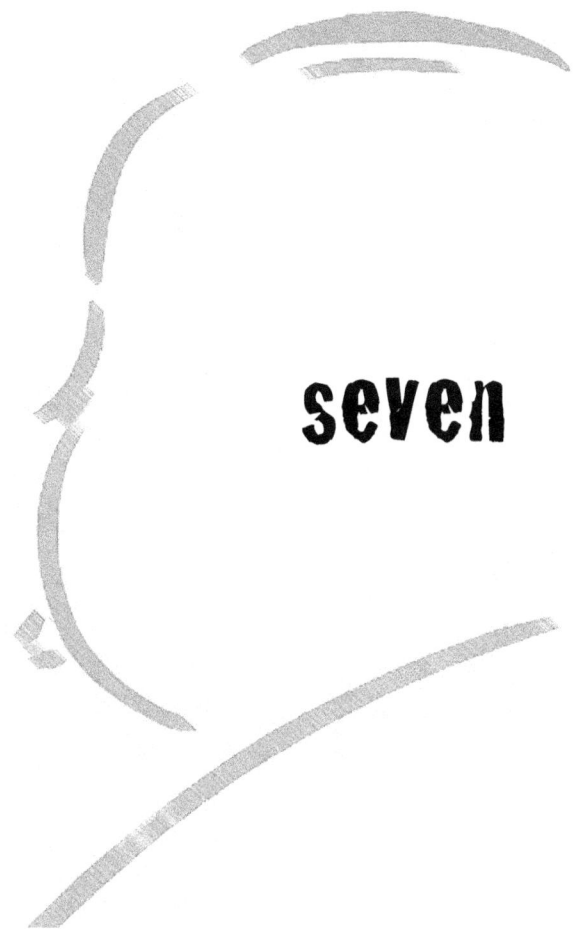

seven

ALFRED HITCHCOCK: the icon years

ALFRED HITCHCOCK: the icon years

"I can hear them screaming when I am making a picture."
Alfred Hitchcock

The Birds

Trying to strike while the iron is hot, Hitchcock returns to the world of horror with his follow-up to 'Psycho'

Alfred Hitchcock's *The Birds* is a culmination of cinematic skills from a director whose success reached far beyond the limits of the movie screen. He became an icon, whose face and name were recognized around the world. He impacted the way films were made and the notoriety of those who made them. Never had a director achieved such notoriety. His classic features tested the boundaries of where film could go and how it could make us feel. By 1960 he was at the peak of his craft and all the tricks he had learned, along with his clout in Hollywood and his keen ability to market and promote his films came together when he embarked on the creation of his 1963 horror classic, *The Birds*.

Follow-up to Success

The Birds was his follow-up film to *Psycho*. *Psycho* had become his biggest hit in a career spanning 40 years. Fans flocked to see it, critics argued over it unable to agree if it was cinematic genius or cheap-shot horror. It broke box office records and has continued to land on top ten lists as one of the greatest films ever. In fact, Hitchcock never really intended it to reach the heights it did. He had seen lesser-known directors lift elements from his films and steal his marketing savvy for their own schlock horror films, so he decided to turn the tables. Using the crew of his TV series and actors who were not well known, except for Janet Leigh, Hitchcock created his own low-budget horror to set the standard for years to come. He had no idea it would become as big as it did.

But after the success of *Psycho*, Hitchcock knew he had to find something compelling to deliver to his audience. He also had the freedom to make his own choices and any studio was glad to have him. He had been considering a dramatic costume drama called *Mary Rose* for some time, and another picture called *Marnie*, but the suspense of *Psycho* would have audiences looking for something equally jarring. He considered but passed on a feature version of David Beaty's novel *Village of Stars*, as he had reportedly purchased the film rights in 1960. The story follows a pilot who is given orders to drop a nuclear bomb. But drama ensues after the orders are aborted and the pilot cannot defuse the bomb. The drama takes place with the plane is in flight and the pilot is trying to avoid nuclear destruction.

Many film historians suggest that Hitchcock knew *The Birds* would follow *Psycho* and included many references to his feathered friends in the film. Janet Leigh's character was named Crane, Anthony Perkins' character, Norman Bates stuffed birds as a hobby, he tells Marion she "eats like a bird" and peers at her through a hole in the wall that is concealed by a painting of birds. Those and other references hint at what was coming – a revenge of the birds.

The Cool Blonde

While he never had the handsome good looks of his leading men, many say his films depict a longing for his leading ladies. In particular, the image of a cool, beautiful blonde emerged as a central figure in many of his most successful films. Grace Kelly, the quintessential Hitchcock leading lady starred in three of the director's most successful pictures, including *Dial M for Murder, To Catch a Thief,* and *Rear Window*. She certainly would have starred in more had she not married the Prince of Monaco, becoming Princess Grace. Other actresses, like Kim Novak in *Vertigo,* Vera Miles in *The Wrong Man*, Eva Marie Saint in *North by Northwest*, Doris Day in *The Man Who Knew Too Much*, and Janet Leigh in *Psycho*, all filled the role of the cool blonde after Kelly left the silver screen. But none captured Hitchcock's eye like Tippi Hedren when he cast her in *The Birds*.

Based on a short story by Daphne du Maurier, the script by Evan Hunter jettisons most of the specifics of the du Maurier story, except for the central plot of flocks of birds attacking people and du Maurier reportedly hated what Hitchcock did to her story. The leading character in Hitchcock's story was again, a cool beautiful blonde. But Hitchcock needed to find her.

In the fall of 1961 Hitchcock and his wife Alma were reportedly watching the *Today* show when he spotted a beautiful young model in a commercial. She was selling a diet drink called Sego and as she walked across the street a boy's whistle caused her to stop, turn and smile. When Hitchcock saw her he decided she could be his next Grace Kelly. In fact, Hitchcock stole the whistle-stopping moment for his opening scene in introducing Hedren to audiences in *The Birds* as she crosses San Francisco's Union Square.

Later that same day Hitchcock told his agents to find out who the beauty was and to set up a meeting with her. Natalie Kay Hedren was located and invited to a meeting at MCA with Hitchcock's agents. She recalled in an interview that it was on October 13, 1961 she received the call. Initially she had no idea Alfred Hitchcock was interested in her. The director's name was never mentioned during the first meeting. It wasn't until a second meeting, several days later that his name came up. Soon after Hedren met with Hitchcock and only thought she was being considered for a small role in one of his TV shows for *Alfred Hitchcock Presents.*

Hedren started out her career as a model in New York. She then decided to give Hollywood and acting as a try and moved to Los Angeles. She was a single mother who in an interview said "I had come to Los Angeles not only to try for better work than what was in New York, but also because I wanted my daughter to grow up in a home with a yard and trees and a neighborhood to roam and play in." Her daughter became actress Melanie Griffith.

Groomed for Stardom

Hedren said the offer from Hitchcock "came at a great time" and she signed a seven-year contract and was groomed for stardom under Alfred Hitchcock. He dropped Natalie as her first name, using her nickname 'Tippi' – a twist on the Swedish term Tupsa, a term of endearment. The name had been given to her by her father and Hitchcock decided it was unique enough to be the perfect screen name. He even put the name in single quote marks to emphasize it. She was then given elaborate screen tests, filming scenes from *To Catch a Thief, Notorious* and *Rebecca* had a wardrobe designed for her by Edith Head to wear when she was off screen as well as on, and he began managing most aspects of her life.

She learned she was to star in Hitchcock's next picture, *The Birds*, a thriller to outshine *Psycho*. The roller coaster ride film centered on a small Northern California town under attack by birds and a number of name actors would be cast in the film, but the real stars of the picture were the birds – and Alfred Hitchcock, of course.

The Birds was a tough film to make – for director and star. Appearing in almost every scene, Hedren was subject to long hours of having birds tossed at her or tied to her. And special effects were used to create some of the more dramatic invasion scenes making it one of Hitchcock's most challenging films from a technical aspect.

Preparing for the Movie

It was in early 1960 when Hitchcock read in the newspaper that a family was attacked by a large number of birds when they flew down the chimney of their home in La Jolla, California. Hitchcock recalled reading the du Maurier short story some years back and dusted it off for another look. He then spent time vacationing and in Europe and to attend various premieres of *Psycho* and returning to Hollywood later in the year.

He continued looking for film projects and working on his TV series when, in the fall of 1961, another bird attack hit headlines after birds attacked a small town near Santa Cruz, California. This time more damage was noted on the town than in the earlier story and Hitchcock began seriously considering that a film about bird attacks could be successful.

After considering several writers for the project Hitchcock settled on Evan Hunter, a novelist and screenwriter who had written books under the name Ed McBain and had also written for Hitchcock's TV series as well as other film and TV projects. Hitchcock felt a novelist could bring life to the characters the story centered on because the short story lacked those elements.

Once the story came together casting began. Rewrites on the script carried on into early 1962. Filming was set to begin in March 1962. With his leading lady in place Hitchcock selected a cast of less-known actors for the other major roles. Aside from the fact that it saved the production money, the cast was not intended to distract audiences from the birds.

Hitchcock had most of the townspeople in Bodega Bay photographed and had many of their outfits and looks copied to make the actors and extras look like the real thing and he based many of the locations on real places in the area including Brinkmeyer's General Store which was based on the real Bodega Bay store called Diekmann's General Store.

Rod Taylor was a young actor who had one of his first major starring roles in *The Birds* as Mitch Brenner. His strong features and good looks mirrored other leading men Hitchcock had cast in prior films, like John Gavin in *Psycho*. Instead of the suggested Anne Bancroft as schoolteacher Annie Hayward, the director selected Suzanne Pleashette who had a long list of credits but wasn't as well known. And for the key role of mother Lydia Brenner, Hitchcock selected renowned stage actress Jessica Tandy, who's talent was well known to other actors, but her name and face were not as well recognized by moviegoers. Veronica Cartwright was cast as Mitch Brenner's younger sister Cathy.

Location shooting was set mostly for Bodega Bay, where the story takes place, but some early shots in San Francisco, including Hitch's cameo, outside a fictional bird shop in downtown Union Square in San Francisco, brought the movie crew to the city. The cast and crew spent most of March and April of 1962 on location in Northern California.

Bodega Bay is a small Northern California town roughly two hours north of San Francisco. For eight weeks the cast and crew worked constantly on location in Bodega Bay. And so many people involved in the filming were being pecked and injured by the birds used in the project that everyone was ordered to receive tetanus shots. The Humane Society was also on hand to make sure the animals were not harmed during the film's production, but no doctor was on set for the actors, Hedren recalled.

Hitchcock reportedly began obsessing over his star Tippi Hedren, preventing her from mingling with other members of the cast and crew. She was taken by car to and from the set alone and would be subjected to lengthy personal sessions with her director.

Others in the cast, including Suzanne Pleshette and Rod Taylor noticed the behavior and commented on it.

During the six weeks in Bodega Bay cast and crew often ate at the Tides Restaurant. In fact, the owner agreed to a deal with Hitchcock, allowing him to use the restaurant in the film at no cost in exchange for giving the owner a cameo appearance and one line in the movie.

Hitch also staged a famous oath with cast and crew outside the restaurant. In front of publicity cameras he has all members of cast and crew swear and oath not to give away the ending of the movie. The oath was merely a media event since the ending of the film wasn't really even known to anyone at that point.

After location shooting another 12 weeks of shooting back in Hollywood was required on soundstages for interior shots and special effects sequences. All in all, the cast spent nearly six months working on the film and the technical crew was required for a year before the project could be completed. Real birds were used for much of the production and the production was fined $400 at one point during filming for having more birds in their possession than allowed by law.

The special effects sequences created a bigger challenge for the director than any of his previous works. In fact, the film reportedly had more than double, or some suggest nearly three times the number of shots of an average Hitchcock film.

Some 1,400 shots are included in the film. Several key sequences required film layers so it would appear birds were attacking the town and its people. Actors were required to act out the attack with no birds in view and later film of birds would be layered intricately overtop the other sequence adding the birds to the scene. Audiences were fooled by the effect and it worked surprisingly well. Hitchcock's second unit crew filmed birds diving for food at various locations including the San Francisco City Dump. At one point overcast weather and fog delayed usable footage from being captured as a crew used up 20,000 feet of film trying to capture gulls for use in an attack scene.

Editing began in July 1962 and carried on tediously through the remainder of the year and into early 1963 when the film was finally completed.

The Release

The first showing of *The Birds* was on March 27, 1963 at the Museum of Modern Art in New York. It was a press screening of the film and the actual release would take place the next day, March 28, 1963. It was also announced that the film would open the Cannes Film Festival in 1963.

In its opening week, *The Birds* was a resounding success with fans lining up to see what Hitchcock had unleashed. Grossing nearly $11.5 million in U.S. box office receipts Universal considered it a blockbuster, although critically it never reached the level of *Psycho*. (Though *Psycho* wasn't received well by critics either.)

It was Hitchcock's first film under a new Universal contract. In fact, in 1963 Universal dropped the word "International" from its name and re-branded itself with a new logo. *The Birds* was the first film to feature the new name and logo. Hitchcock's longtime friend and agent Lew Wasserman was one of the top heads at the studio and gave Hitchcock the freedom to choose his projects and have virtually complete control over the productions. It sounded too good to be true. And in some cases, Hitch would find out later that it was. But financially, it would turn out to be a smart move and it would make Hitchcock a very wealthy man.

As for *The Birds*, critics didn't particularly warm up to the film. While it was highly regarded for its technical achievements, some found the story lacking and didn't rate the film as highly as *Psycho*. In reality, many of those same critics had at first disregarded *Psycho* as inferior as well, later reevaluating the film as a classic.

Some critics criticized the acting, while others felt the story lacked substance and the resolution of the film left some wondering what it was all for. Arthur Knight of *Saturday's Review* said the story "gets off to an incredibly slow start, embellishing the introduction of the principals with all sorts of unnecessary and tedious details." *Variety* called it a "Hitchcock-and-bull story that's essentially a fowl ball" while *Time* magazine felt the feathered fiends were "terrifyingly believable as they go about their bloody business of murdering humanity."

However, Hitchcock intentionally ended the film on a very ambiguous note by having the film conclude with merely a scene of the main characters driving off and a mass of birds as far as the eye could see. It was an attempt to appeal to more auteur film critics and French filmmakers who would often leave moviegoers guessing what was next. In fact Hitch even refused to put "The End" at the conclusion of the picture to leave viewers a bit uneasy and on edge as they left the theater. It was an attempt at trying to present his films as a work of art from an icon and not just a movie.

Some reports suggest Hitch considered several different endings to the film including one where the Brenner clan reach San Francisco only to find the Golden Gate Bridge covered with birds. Hitch was now beginning to think of the legacy he would leave behind.

After The Birds

After *The Birds* Hitchcock was very much in favor of continuing his association with Tippi Hedren as he felt she had much to offer the camera. But he also toyed with another project during this period.

Trap for a Solitary Man was intended to be a Hitchcock picture filmed in Cinemascope for Twentieth Century Fox. It was based on a French play by M. Robert Thomas that follows a young married couple who go on holiday in the French Alps. During their vacation the wife disappears, and the distraught husband contacts the police and they begin a lengthy search for his missing wife.

When they bring back a woman who they claim is her, his hopes are dashed when the man doesn't recognize her. He says he's never seen her before in his life because she is not his wife. But when the woman claims she is the man's wife, things take an unusual twist. The film would never be directed by Hitch and he would again abandon a project in favor of another.

He would do it again in 1964 when Hitchcock considered turning another novel into film when he read *The Three Hostages* by John Buchan. The suspense comes when the leading man is hypnotized by the blind mother of the story's villain. Hitchcock, according to some interviews, didn't think the story line of the hypnosis would not be believable with moviegoers and he gave up on the concept. But he had another project in mind and his leading lady had already proved herself.

ALFRED HITCHCOCK: the icon years

eight

ALFRED HITCHCOCK: the icon years

ALFRED HITCHCOCK: the icon years

"As you will have seen, murder seems to be the prominent theme."

Alfred Hitchcock

MOMA Exhibition

Hitchcock's icon status further cemented by Museum of Modern Art retrospective

The evening prior to the New York premiere of *The Birds*, New York's Museum of Modern Art held a press screening of the film. Not only was this a coup for the director to help promote his latest release, but the event would also help him in his aim to be taken seriously as an artist. Alfred Hitchcock was thinking about the legacy of work he would leave behind.

ALFRED HITCHCOCK: the icon years

Hitchcock had achieved success at the box office and with the critics many times, but he also wanted to be remembered as a serious filmmaker of artistic notoriety. He was beginning to think about his legacy. Filmmakers like Henri-Georges Clouzot, Roberto Rossellini, Roman Polanski, Billy Wilder, Orson Welles, Stanley Kubrick, John Frankenheimer and others were considered artists, while Hitchcock's pop-culture status often seemed to prevent him from elevation to the same space. While they may have envied his success and longevity he longed to have his films respected for their artistic value.

Films of Artistic Merit

Having a major art museum premiere his latest work was a great step in the direction of having his work viewed for its artistic merit. In fact, that was just the beginning. It was with this screening that the museum announced that it was preparing a major retrospective of Hitchcock's larger body of work. While the museum was most often known for focusing on films that addressed social or economic ills and issues, Hitchcock's reputation as the master of suspense and his status as America's most beloved director – and television star – gave them reason to reconsider him as an American master of cinema.

Still, it was somewhat surprising because Richard Griffith, head of MOMA's film program at the time, actually held no fondness whatsoever for Hitchcock or his work. He reportedly found *Vertigo* "lacking in substance" and wrote of Hitchcock's limitations in 1951 by saying "This specialist in mystery stories needed no roots in national life for the kind of entertainment he purveyed."

However, Griffith had arranged several other film retrospectives – one for Orson Welles in 1961 and another for Howard Hawkes in 1962. Film critic, journalist and soon-to-be director Peter Bogdanavich was the brainchild behind the event. He originally proposed the idea to a New York repertory theater, but the cost of mounting such a showing was far too great so Bogdanovich approached the MOMA.

After he brought in the New York publicity firm that was handling the promotion of *The Birds* Bogdanovich was able to get the PR firm to cover the costs of the entire retrospective as part of Universal's promotion for *The Birds*, which certainly pleased Griffith. The museum was then given the opportunity to exhibit a series of Hitchcock films over a six-month period at no cost, allowing them to pull in a wide range of moviegoers that would offer a broader pop-culture demographic than the usual art-goer they attracted.

On March 29, 1963 *The New York Times* reported the MOMA exhibit by writing "Alfred Hitchcock's movies will be the subject of the longest retrospective ever held at the museum." The report went on to say that the series was "arranged by Richard Griffith, film curator at MOMA and one of the leading historians of the movie industry."

Hitchcock himself offered his own statement on news of the retrospective saying, "I am happy and honored to present *The Birds* at the festival inauguration. I consider it a masterpiece in every sense of the word."

While *The Birds* wouldn't achieve the level of success of his prior film, Hitchcock would be applauded the special effects and technical achievements and the thrills and suspense of the story would captivate audiences. Had *The Birds* been released prior to *Psycho,* one never knows how well the film would have fared among film historians. But the comparisons to *Psycho* certainly impacted the film's long-term standing.

ALFRED HITCHCOCK: the icon years

ALFRED HITCHCOCK: the icon years

nine

ALFRED HITCHCOCK: the icon years

ALFRED HITCHCOCK: the icon years

The length of a film should be directly related to the endurance of the human bladder."

Alfred Hitchcock

Marnie

Obsession casts a shadow over Alfred Hitchcock's "most personal" film

Hitchcock would move into a darker phase as the 60s wore on. With three of his most financially rewarding films behind him, his success as a filmmaker having arguably peaked with the release of *Psycho* in 1960, the director would struggle to meet public and critical expectation surrounding his films as well as differentiate himself from the horror-suspense films he had become known for after his last two box office outings. It would be a struggle he would endure for the rest of his career and his life.

With *North by Northwest* taking Hitchcock out of the 50s on a high note and Hitchcock rocking the movie world with the immense success of *Psycho,* the director had achieved even greater notoriety than even he expected. When he followed *Psycho* with another big horror-related suspense classic in *The Birds* he managed to keep critics and moviegoers on edge. By 1964 everyone wondered what he possibly could have up his sleeve as an encore.

He was known as the master of suspense, and as one of Hollywood's best known and most successful directors, Hitchcock made himself a star in a way few directors would ever achieve. While his motion pictures continue to delight fans and create discussion through books, magazine articles, television and documentaries, for Hitchcock, popularity and acclaim were a path to acceptance for an insecure man who never was fully comfortable in his own skin. In fact, his security came mainly from the world he created on film and the financial security it provided him, while insecurity was a major part of his waking reality.

Hitchcock's ordinary looks and his battles with his weight never provided him with the handsome good looks of his leading men, but his longing for his leading ladies was evident in many of the director's greatest films and became even more evident as his career progressed and his popularity grew.

Hitchcock's Leading Lady

In his later years, the image of a cool, beautiful but icy blonde emerged as a central figure in many of his films. Grace Kelly, perhaps the quintessential Hitchcock leading lady, starred in three of the director's most successful films – *Dial M For Murder, Rear Window* and *To Catch a Thief.* She certainly would have starred in more had she not married the Prince of

ALFRED HITCHCOCK: the icon years

Monaco to become Princess Grace. Kim Novak in *Vertigo*, Doris Day in *The Man Who Knew Too Much*, Vera Miles in *The Wrong Man*, Eva Marie Saint in *North By Northwest* and Janet Leigh in *Psycho*, all to some extent filled that role, although none captured Hitchcock's eye quite the way as Kelly had. Not until Tippi Hedren.

In Hedren, Hitchcock saw a beauty that spelled star and an actress he could build into his replacement for Grace Kelly. Many saw the similarities between the looks of the two women, but Hedren was undiscovered. She would go on to star in two pictures for Hitchcock – one would be one of his biggest hits, *The Birds*. The other has been noted as one of his greatest failures. The film was *Marnie*.

The plans Hitchcock had for Hedren and the production problems he faced during the making of *Marnie* made for a doomed production that spelled disaster for both the director and the star. And the film has been examined and reexamined for years for both its impact on screen and off. Critics and fans alike are still unable to come to a conclusion on the worthiness of *Marnie* within Hitchcock's body of work.

But the film was a defining moment within the career of Alfred Hitchcock and in some ways became a turning point for the director. It also offers us a lasting impression of the talent of Tippi Hedren and the actress she was becoming.

As previously mentioned, it was in the fall of 1961 when Hitchcock first became aware of Tippi Hedren. Hitchcock quickly became fascinated by her beauty and set out to find her and sign her to a seven-year contract.

She was groomed for stardom with elaborate screen tests, a specially designed wardrobe for both on and off the set and he spent time instructing and tutoring her on how to become the star he envisioned. While *The Birds* was a tough picture for the director it was probably tougher on its leading lady. But she came through with flying colors and in the end it paid off at the box office. The movie made millions in the spring of 1963.

But even so, critics didn't regard it as highly as *Psycho*, but recognized the film for its technical achievements and found it a suitable follow-up to his greatest hit.

Difficult Task of Topping The Birds

For a follow-up to *The Birds*, the task again was a daunting one. Similar to *Psycho*, he had achieved a box office hit that delighted fans and set himself up with an audience expecting nothing less than amazing. Hitchcock had been considering a book by Winston Graham. *Marnie* had actually been viewed as a vehicle for Grace Kelly who was considering a return to the big screen.

In a statement issued by the Royal Palace in Monaco in March 1962, it was announced that Princess Grace would "play the lead in Hitchcock's new film *Marnie*." But apparently no one asked her public first. The public outcry in Monaco was immense as many found the idea of their princess returning to Hollywood to make a movie a very tasteless idea. The story also began to fuel rumors that the fairy tale marriage of the prince and the movie star was on the rocks.

The princess ultimately decided her return to films would not be realized. Another factor that helped sway her was the fact that when Grace Kelly left Hollywood to become a princess she had more than four years left on her studio contract with MGM. And while it was bad publicity for MGM to make a big deal out of the issue while the star was retired and serving the people of Monaco, it was another thing if she was starring in a major motion picture for Universal. There were threats of legal action even after the actress announced that her salary would be donated to several children's charities. She eventually decided it was best to decline the role. The picture was put off until Hitchcock found a suitable star as he focused his attention on *The Birds*.

After signing Hedren to a seven-year contract at $500 a week and seeing early footage of her in *The Birds*, Hitchcock decided she could fill Kelly's shoes and assigned her to the leading role in *Marnie*. Hedren passed all Hitchcock's tests and was a bargain under her contract.

By the time *Marnie* was in pre-production Hedren was already worried about the constant supervision by Hitchcock. He kept his star from socializing with fellow cast members and supposedly gave the cameraman instructions to bring the camera as close to Hedren's face as possible. Telling the cameraman that the lenses were "almost to make love to the star."

He asked crew members from the set to trail her outside the studio and report back to him her every move. According to one biographer he even reportedly had her handwriting analyzed to see if there was anything in her personality that might tell of hidden desires for her director that she hid with coolness. While nothing was noted, Hitchcock's fascination with his star continued to grow.

During the filming of key scenes the director invited studio executives to the set to see what he referred to as his "ultimate actress." Hitchcock believed she was giving an Academy Award performance and spoke strongly of his feelings for her. "They were not surprised of the feelings," wrote one biographer. "They were astounded as his admission of them."

As the months wore on Hedren began to grow frustrated and angry. The cast and crew sensed the discomfort on the set but production continued as all tried to avoid tension and finish the film. And during filming, Hitchcock also began pre-production work on his next picture, *Mary Rose*, which he would again star Hedren. But before *Mary Rose* could be filmed tension on the set of *Marnie* would reach a boiling point and the relationship between director and star would reportedly turn ugly.

Sexual Tension Reaches a Boiling Point

Filming on *Marnie* neared completion and after months of watching her, directing her life on and off the set, and subjecting her to reported uncomfortable sexual innuendos, the director finally went too far. Alone in Hedren's trailer after a day of filming, Hitchcock reportedly made a sexual proposition to Hedren that she could not ignore casually, as she had the director's previous remarks.

Reports said that Hedren was a first shocked by his forwardness and directly refused his advances making it clear to the director that she had no intention of ever being involved with him in any other way than as an actress under his direction. She said she'd had all she could take and had reached her limit. Hitchcock, it was said, was furious and possibly embarrassed. And being spurned by the actress he was making into a star was a blow to his ego. It was many years before sexual harassment would be a commonly-used term and at the time it seemed there was little actresses could do when faced with such issues. But Hedren decided to put a stop to it regardless of the repercussions.

Now some say this exchange never occurred and dispute the tale. But regardless there was a definite parting of the ways between Hedren and Hitchcock at this time. One rumor was that Hedren made a comment about the director's weight and he became incensed. Hedren denies this. She explained at one point that it was his refusal to allow her to accept a *Photoplay* award on national television for Most Promising New Actress in 1964 that caused an angry confrontation between the two and resulted in the distance between them.

Whatever the cause, Hitchcock cancelled his plans to film *Mary Rose*. He apparently then cut her salary and was rumored to have stopped talking to the actress directly. He would only refer to her as "that girl."

He would attempt to ruin her career by only offering her small roles on television since she was still under contract and he refused to loan her out for other major roles she was offered. He also lost all interest in *Marnie* as if he even wanted the film to fail.

He stopped focusing on the technical details of the film and the editing process as a whole. He refused others' advice on potential reworking of the film and some of the rear projection shots and special effects. He retreated to his home, only occasionally visiting the studio to check on the progress of the editing.

When the film was finally released in 1964 it was rated a critical and financial failure for both the director and Hedren. *Time* magazine said of the movie, "When an unknown director turns out a suspense yarn melodrama as dreary and unconvincing as this, moviegoers reveal the thought of what it might have been if Hitchcock had done it. It is disconcerting to come away from *Marnie* feeling precisely the same way."

Many critics panned the initial release and fans rejected the picture as well. Audiences expected a suspense feature that would out-do *The Birds* or offer the thrills of *Psycho*. Hedren and co-star Sean Connery were singled out for "lackluster" performances.

The film fared poorly at the box office by Universal's expectations. With smashes for his last few films it was expected any movie he released would do well. At a budget of roughly $3 million, the movie actually only pulled in about $7 million. Some blamed Hitchcock's disinterest and lack of promotion.

In fact, Hitchcock offered minimal personal promotion of the film and gave little support to its star. Had he the outcome may have been quite different. But Hitchcock was finished with Tippi Hedren.

Hitchcock handed over Hedren's contact to Universal, but when she reportedly refused to work in a Universal TV series, the contract was torn up. But by then the damage was done. Hitchcock refused to allow her to star in a film being produced by Francois Truffaut and his *Mary Rose* project, much like *No Bail for the Judge*, would never be made.

With or without Hedren, like his experience with Audrey Hepburn, his disappointment caused him to lose interest in the film altogether, though he at first tried to move ahead. The roles that Hedren was offered after this were small or in mediocre productions.

ALFRED HITCHCOCK: the icon years

Hedren Moves On

According to Francois Truffaut who conducted a series of interviews with Hitchcock in the late 60s and early 1970s the director refused to discuss his relationship with Hedren. In addition, after *Marnie*, the image of a cool beautiful blonde would seldom again appear in a Hitchcock picture and would never be the center of it.

With regards to her relationship to Hitchcock, Hedren said in a 1994 interview, "An obsession is what it was. It's a very miserable situation to be the object of someone's obsession. It's very confining, very frightening and I didn't like it."

Hedren married and raised her daughter, actress Melanie Griffith, and occasionally worked in films and television. Her films include *A Countess From Hong Kong, Pacific Heights,* and *Through the Eyes of a Killer.* She was also active in television with several TV movies, a role on cable series *Dream On*, and in the soap opera *The Bold and the Beautiful.* She also returned for a cable-made sequel to Hitchcock's *The Birds – Lands End* in the 1990s.

But Hedren's biggest accomplishment since her work with Hitchcock has been the development of the Shambala Preserve, a 60-acre ranch in Acton, California where some 68 large animals, including leopards, mountain lions, Bengal and Siberian tigers, African lions and elephants roam free. Hedren has been honored with numerous awards for her efforts and uses her celebrity to raise awareness of the treatment of animals and endangered species. Her film and TV work is also used to help support the foundation financially. The preserve itself came about after Hedren filmed the movie *Roar* because some of the animals used in the film were in need of a home.

Of Hitchcock she said, "I've seen most of Hitch's movies and I've read some biographies but I'm not sure I ever knew the real Hitchcock. Perhaps no one did."

ALFRED HITCHCOCK: the icon years

It's important to note that not everyone supports the theory of Hitchcock as a director obsessed with his leading ladies. Janet Leigh, who starred in *Psycho* and Kim Novak from *Vertigo*, both recalled working with Hitchcock fondly with no signs of difficulty.

As for *Marnie*, much has been written and said. While still not regarded as Hitchcock's greatest accomplishment, some regard it as the director's most personal film, with its troubled sexual themes and duel personalities. *Marnie* has been reevaluated for its rich vision and deep story, filled with turmoil and mystery that seems all the more interesting knowing the circumstances under which it was created.

In 1986, on the release of the film on video *The Chicago Tribune* wrote, "*Marnie*, with its astonishingly naked, vulnerable performance by Tippi Hedren, is almost the most emotionally open of all Hitchcock's films ... A dense, beautiful film, it well rewards the multiple viewings made possible by home video."

Hitchcock Moves on As Well

After seven seasons of *Alfred Hitchcock Presents* and three seasons of *The Alfred Hitchcock Hour*, Alfred Hitchcock's TV presence would come to a close in 1965. In fact, it would be an anti-climactic event, with NBC never even releasing a statement to announce the show's cancellation. They just chose not to renew his series and CBS didn't express interest either. The last show aired in May 1965.

The ratings of *The Alfred Hitchcock Hour* had slipped, although not dramatically. It was reported that NBC felt the show was "a little too costly" for what it returned in ratings. But Hitchcock wasn't all that distraught by the end. Hitchcock friend Norman Lloyd said "The real reason was that Hitch didn't want to do it anymore. He felt that ten years was enough, and he had a lot of other things to do."

Hitch himself said of the show's cancellation, "We must be philosophical about this. As we all know, television is a great juggernaut and we're all nuts and bolts attached to it. Sometimes the nuts and bolts fall off."

But when it came to his bank account, the show proved to be a wise move. In 1964, he sold the rights to both the series and his hit film *Psycho* to MCA in exchange for approximately 150,000 shares of MCA stock. The deal would make him the Universal's third-largest shareholder and give him the clout he would need to continue making films for the remainder of his career.

ALFRED HITCHCOCK: the icon years

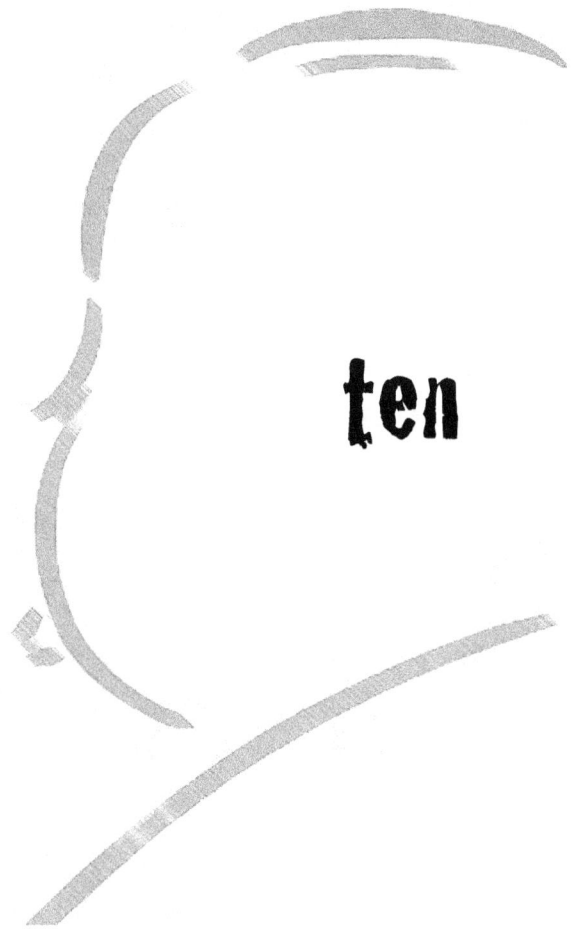

ten

ALFRED HITCHCOCK: the icon years

ALFRED HITCHCOCK: the icon years

"A good film is when the price of the dinner, the theatre admission and the babysitter were worth it."

Alfred Hitchcock

The Saga of Mary Rose

Hitchcock's unfinished ghost story

Back in 1920, while living in London and still very early in his career, Alfred Hitchcock spent a great deal of time at the theater. In fact, during these years, according to several reports, he saw nearly every major play in London. It would be several years before he would begin directing his collection of legendary films, but as a member of the crew on a handful of silent films and as a would-be writer Hitchcock was immersed in the British entertainment industry learning all he could.

ALFRED HITCHCOCK: the icon years

That year he saw a play called *Mary Rose* as London's Haymarket Theatre. It starred a young woman named Fay Compton, who Hitch would later work with on his first and only attempt at a musical, *Waltzes of Vienna* when he cast her as a countess. *Mary Rose* was written by James M. Barrie and would be revived several more times, in 1926, 1929, again in 1951 and more recently in 2007. Hitchcock found himself taken with the story.

The lead title character, Mary Rose, is a teenager when the play opens. She lives at home with her parents, but shortly after the story opens a man named Simon comes to her home to ask her parents for their daughter's hand in marriage. Her parents, Mr. and Mrs. Morley, approve the union but only after explaining to Simon that Mary is "a little different." They tell him that some years earlier, while on vacation in Scotland's Outer Herbides Mary disappeared. Her father was fishing while she was quietly sketching and when he looked back for her after a few moments she was suddenly gone. They looked everywhere for her, but she was nowhere to be found until 30 days later when she reappeared. She had no recollection of having been gone for 30 days and believed that no more than a few hours had passed for her.

The family returned home, but Mary seemed slightly different to them. They could not quite put their finger on it, but her mother explains it to Simon by saying, "I have sometimes thought that our girl is curiously young for her age – as if – you know how just a touch of frost may stop the growth of a plant and yet leave it blooming – it has sometimes seemed to me that a cold finger had once touched my Mary Rose."

Unconcerned about the story, Simon responds by saying, "What you are worrying about is just her innocence - which seems a holy thing to me." He still very much wishes to marry the young girl and the wedding goes forward. About five years later, a married Mary and Simon return to the island with their young son and Mary once again disappears. Mary eventually returns, but this time it's more than 25 years later. Strangely enough, in her return she appears not to have aged more than a day. Her parents and husband, much older now, are confused as is Mary, because she believes no time has passed and expects her three-year-old son to still be a small child. But he, in fact, is a grown man. The son, named Harry, is apparently also now missing. In the original version of the story it is suggested that he is a prisoner of war during World War I.

Harry eventually resurfaces and returns to his childhood home many years later only to find a ghost inhabits the house. He soon discovers that the ghost is that of his mother Mary and the two finally meet again and have a long and touching reunion that sets her free from her ghostly wanderings. She can then return to the island for eternity.

Hitchcock's Movie Version

After seeing the play Hitchcock was captivated by the mysteriousness of the tale and felt the story would make a fine film. He carried the idea with him for many years, eventually buying the screen rights to the play, and in the late 50s and early 60s began to work on the idea as a feature film. In fact it was in the early 60s that he sought out Fay Compton, star of the original theatrical version he saw in 1920, hoping to possibly cast her in one of the roles in his film, perhaps Mary's aged mother.

He hired Jay Presson Allen, the writer who helped breath life into *Marnie* to craft the screen version of the play. A first draft offered Hitchcock the bones of the story and he complemented them with his own ideas for Presson Allen to incorporate into a second draft that she delivered to the director by Valentine's Day 1964.

Albert Whitlock, a longtime collaborator of Hitchcock's was contracted for a number of "sketches" of scenes for the would-be film. Hitchcock once told Whitlock his concept behind the film was to center on the ghostly aspect of Barrie's original story. Hitchcock told him that the film would not be promoted as "Hitchcock's Mary Rose" but as "A Ghost Story by Alfred Hitchcock: Mary Rose." "That'll get 'em," Hitchcock suggested.

His Leading Lady

Hitchcock had at one time reportedly hoped to have Grace Kelly take on the role of Mary Rose and then later set his hopes on his leading lady of *The Birds* and *Marnie*, Tippi Hedren, as the cool beautiful star of the film. But before *Marnie* could make it to the theaters Hedren and Hitchcock would have a falling out. Hedren was dropped as the would-be star of his upcoming *Mary Rose*.

However, Hitch didn't entirely abandon *Mary Rose* once Hedren exited his life. Initially, he kept hope alive of doing the film with another actress. Claire Griswold, was reportedly suggested as his other potential star of the film. The bulk of Griswold's body of work was in television. She would have guest roles on many television dramas in the late 50s and early 60s, including *The DuPont Show of the Month, Perry Mason, The Dick Powell Show* and *The Twilight Zone*. In addition, she would come to Hitchcock's attention through two performances in his TV series, one in 1962 and another in 1963. She too, like Tippi Hedren, would be put through elaborate screen tests, filming scenes from *To Catch a Thief*.

He described his upcoming film to *The Times of London* during a visit to the United Kingdom in 1964 as, "The island that likes to be visited. 'I see it essentially as a horror story.' To hear him describing effects he has in mind for the latter, like having the semi-phantom *Mary Rose* lit from inside, so that she casts a ghostly glow instead of a shadow on the walls, and in a death scene letting her husband feel her brow when she goes into a trance and finds his hand covered in blue powder, 'I don't know exactly what it signifies, but I like the idea', one is left in no doubt that he starts his films very much from the visual end of things."

However, the film was not to be. Claire Griswold, like Grace Kelly, Audrey Hepburn and Vera Miles, would disappoint the director when she chose family over stardom and she would announce her pregnancy before further details of the film could be finalized. He was not pleased.

In addition, the disappointment of *Marnie* left Universal feeling less than enthusiastic about the screenplay of *Mary Rose*. There were too many similarities in the mood and style of the film. And the screenplay, some have said, left out too many ghostly scares that might make for good box office. His horror efforts like *Psycho* and *The Birds* centered on the horrific to sell the pictures and without that his fans were often left disappointed. Lew Wasserman, a key figure as Universal and ardent supporter of Hitchcock wasn't convinced the film would make money.

Hitchcock still had hopes his reputation would help him see the film through and his hopes were boosted when The Screen Producers Guild gave him with their Milestone Award in 1965. Even though *Marnie* had suffered in both reviews and at the box office his renowned as a director still earned him a great deal of respect and admiration. But Universal wasn't about to bankroll another failed experiment, no matter how much of an icon Alfred Hitchcock was and his plans for the film languished.

A Major Disappointment

Hitchcock would later say in interviews that his contract with Universal allowed him to make any film, "so long as it cost under $3 million, and so long as it wasn't *Mary Rose*." But he never stopped thinking about his film version of the story. Hitchcock would detail his idea of the film to Francois Truffaut during his series of interviews in 1967, calling it "a little like a science-fiction story."

"If I were to make the film, I would put the girl in a dark-gray dress and I would put a neon tube of light inside, around the bottom of the dress, so that the light would only hit the heroine. Whenever she moved, there would be no shadow on the wall, only a blue light. You'd have to create the impression of photographing a presence rather than a body. At times she would appear very small in the image, at times very big. She wouldn't be a solid lump, you see, but rather like a sensation. In this way you lose the feeling of real space and time. You should be feeling that you are in the presence of an ephemeral thing, you see."

"It's a lovely subject," commented Truffaut. "Also a sad one."

"Yes, very sad," Hitchcock agreed. "Because the real theme is: If the dead were to come back, what would you do with them?"

Hitchcock continued to believe in the film, telling Truffaut, "I still haven't definitely dropped the idea of making it. A few years back it might have seemed that the story would be too irrational for the public. But since then the public's been exposed to these twilight-zone stories, especially on television …"

In fact, Hitchcock kept the idea of filming *Mary Rose* with him until his death. His estate held the screen rights to the play until 1987, many years after his death.

ALFRED HITCHCOCK: the icon years

By the end of the 1950s Alfred Hitchcock was one of the most familiar faces around the world. From his hit films, to his TV series, his paperback books and his magazines, he was a well-known and sought after commodity.

ALFRED HITCHCOCK: the icon years

Hitchcock branded himself in print with a series of successful paperback books from Dell Publishing.

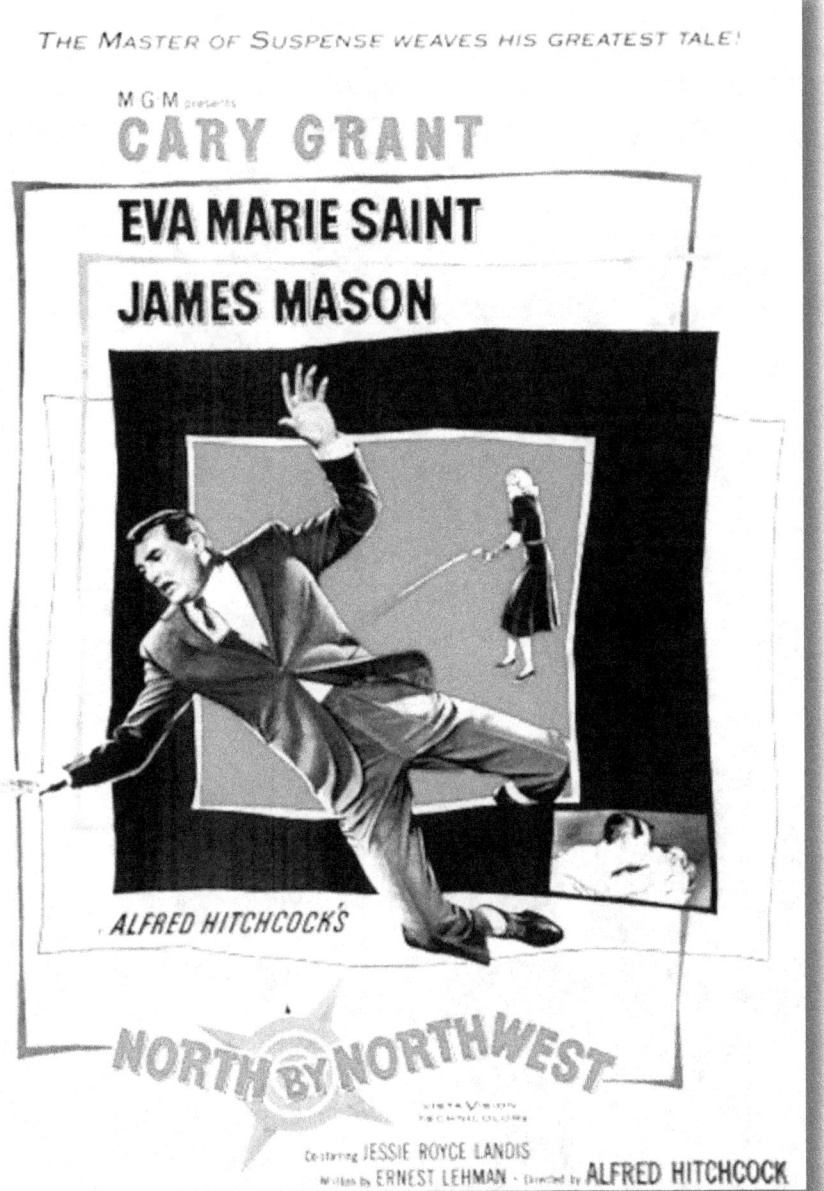

'North by Northwest' in 1959 starring Cary Grant and Eva Marie Saint would become one of the director's most financially successful and critically-acclaimed films and would end the 1950s on a high note, but the director struggled as he looked for a suitable follow-up feature.

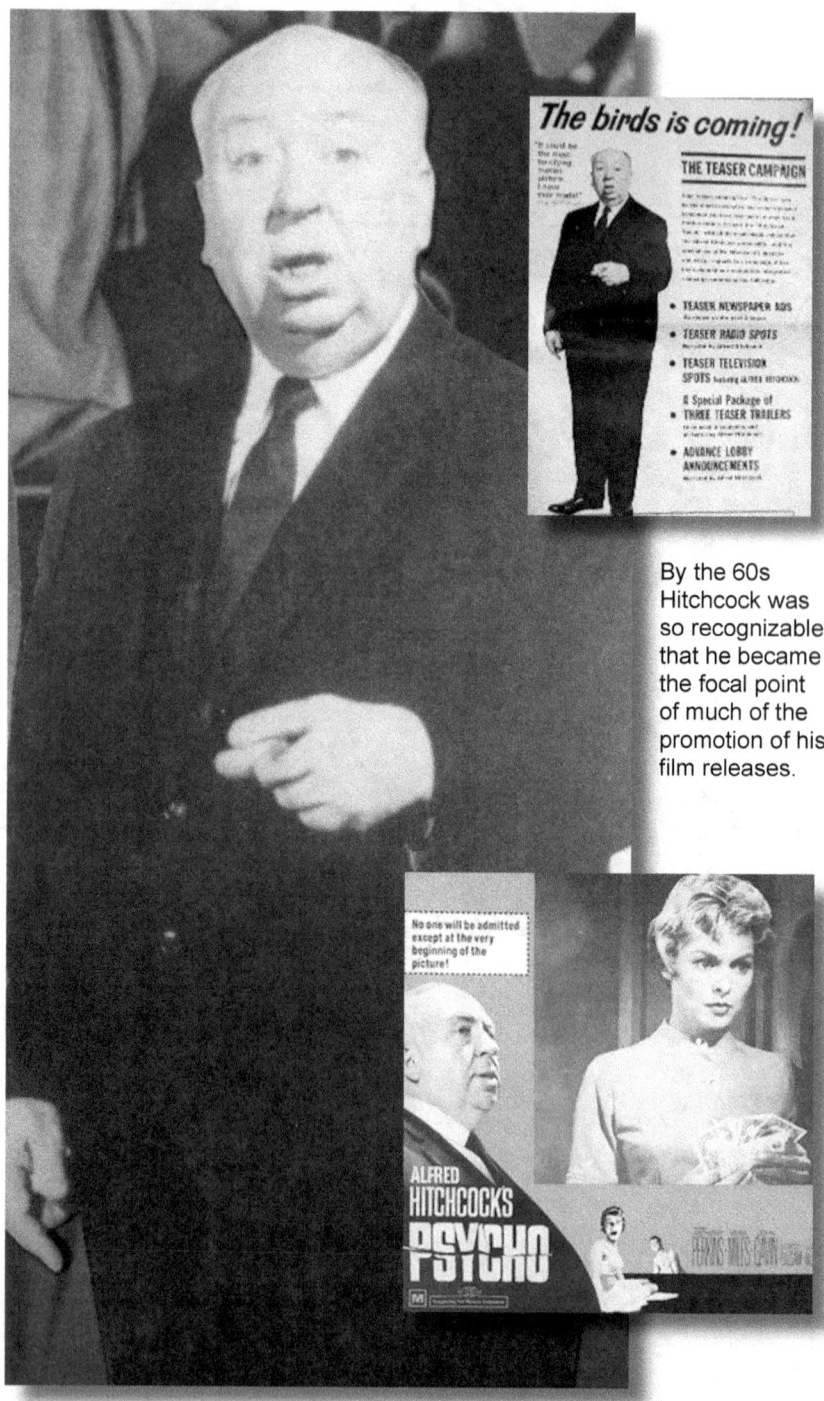

By the 60s Hitchcock was so recognizable that he became the focal point of much of the promotion of his film releases.

ALFRED HITCHCOCK: the icon years

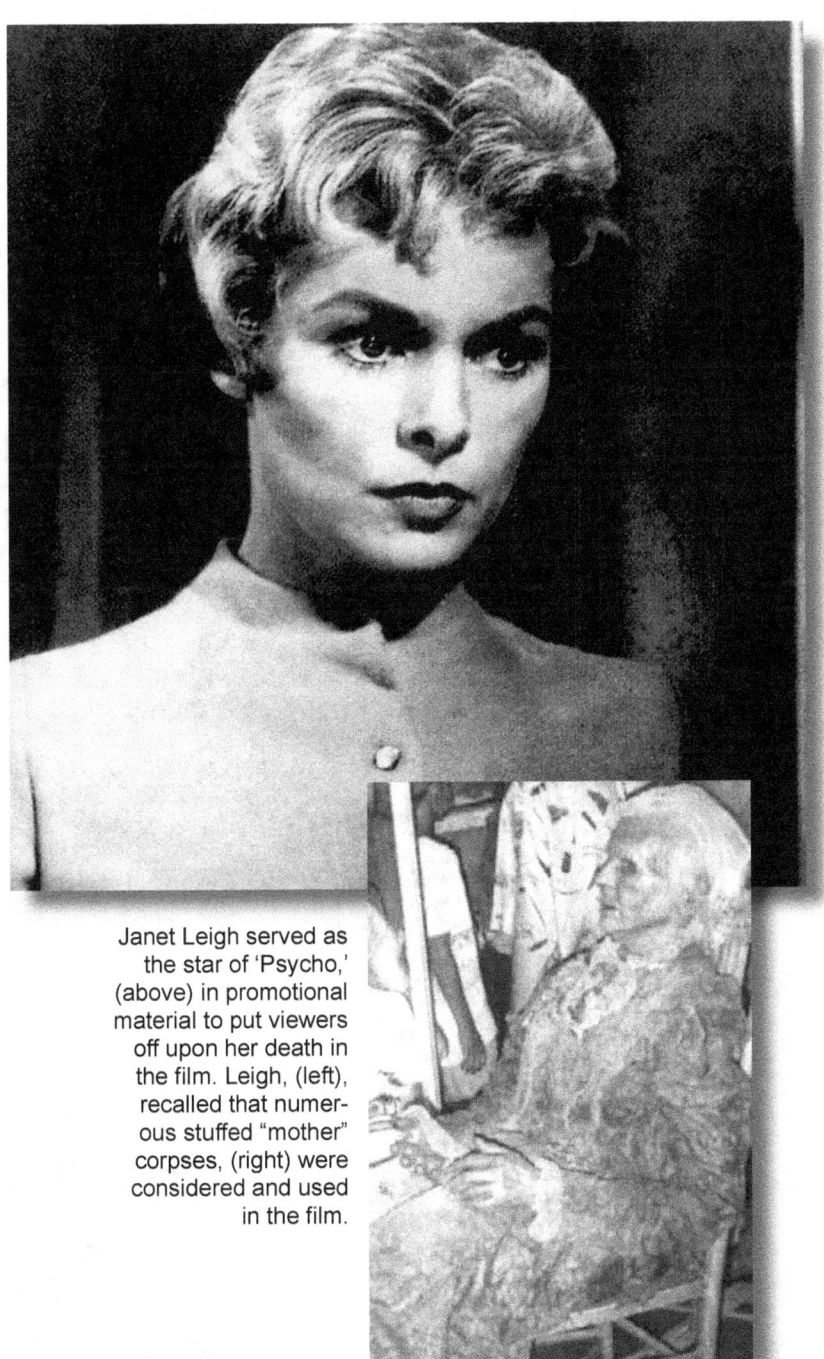

Janet Leigh served as the star of 'Psycho,' (above) in promotional material to put viewers off upon her death in the film. Leigh, (left), recalled that numerous stuffed "mother" corpses, (right) were considered and used in the film.

ALFRED HITCHCOCK: the icon years

Janet Leigh's famous shower scene was filmed over the course of seven days. In later years Leigh would claim she continued to receive odd death threats that stemmed from the scene.

ALFRED HITCHCOCK: the icon years

The release of 'Psycho' in June 1960 was a blockbuster. Theaters (above) were sold out and long lines formed as patrons waited for their chance to see what Hitchcock had created. The infamous house (right) was a set Hitchcock created to offer the eerie home for Norman Bates and his mother. The house remained on the Universal backlot for many years.

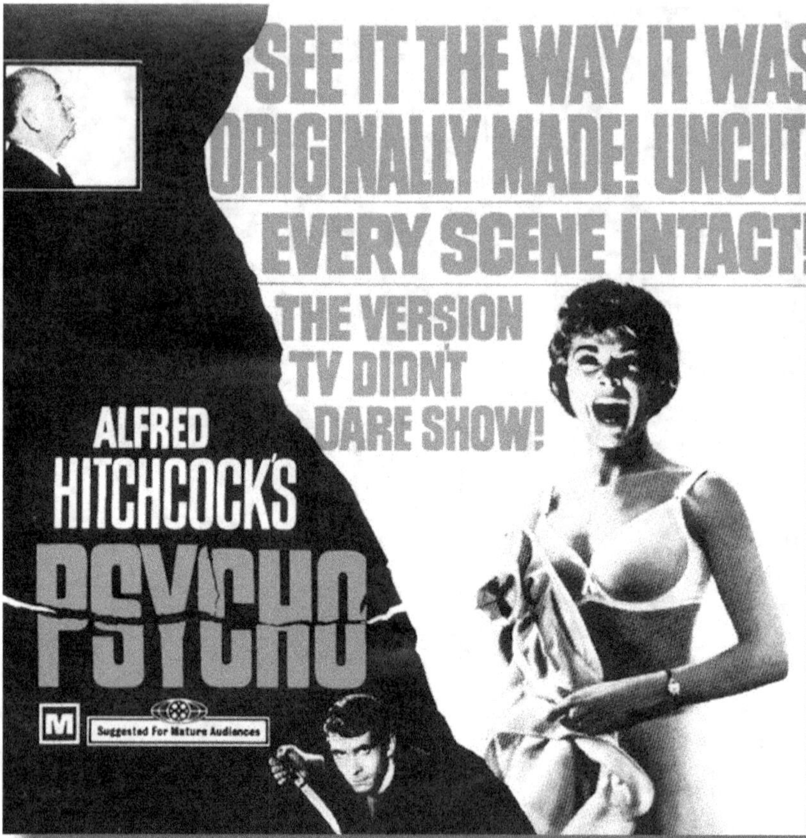

'Psycho' would be released in theaters numerous times after 1960 finding new audiences and bringing new profits to both Universal and the director. A poster (above) promoting one of the re-releases promised to show the version without cuts from a TV broadcast. Vera Miles (left) would reprise her role as Lila in the sequel some 20 years later. Miles had worked with Hitchcock numerous times, including appearances in 'The Wrong Man' and his TV series. She was at one time the intended star for 'Vertigo.'

ALFRED HITCHCOCK: the icon years

Hitchcock on the set of his 1960 classic 'Psycho'.

ALFRED HITCHCOCK: the icon years

Alfred Hitchcock enjoyed putting himself in the spotlight of his motion pictures rather than many of his stars. This became increasingly common during his iconic years of the 1960s and 1970s. Here he poses for a publicity shot for his 1963 film, 'The Birds'.

In her first major film role, Tippi Hedren was cast as the leading lady for Hitchcock's 1963 suspense horror film, 'The Birds', but the director and his thousands of feathered friends were the real stars of the picture.

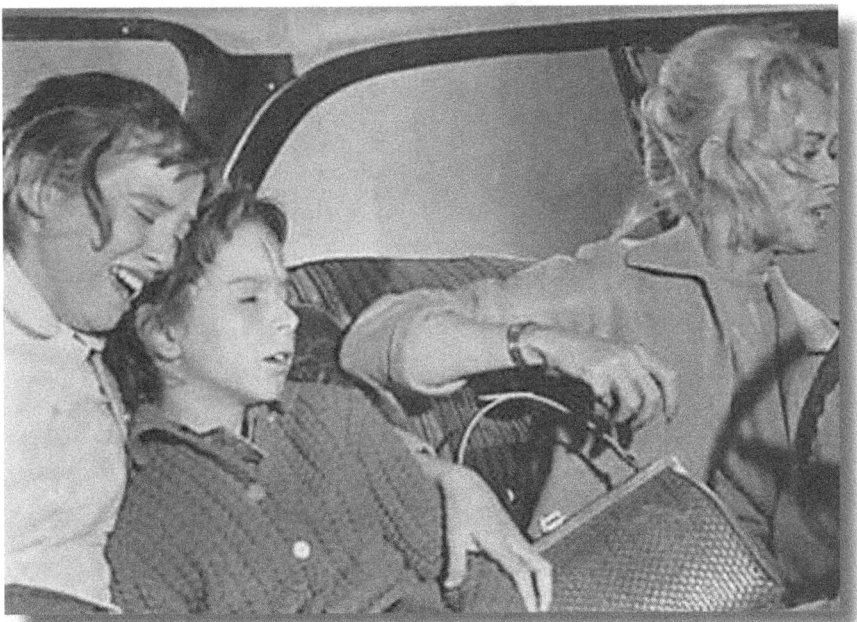

Tippi Hedren was in nearly every scene of 'The Birds' and by the climax of picture she was subjected to a major attack in which birds were tied to her and thrown at her while the director tried to capture a terrifying sequence.

Hitchcock and Universal knew they had a good shot at a hit with a follow-up film to 'Psycho,' but they provided theater owners with tips and instruction to capitalize on the promotional materials they provided them.

Hitchcock toyed with the media in his promotion of the film but promised to offer attacks from 'The Birds.' Tippi Hedren poses with Hitch in one of the promotional shots for the film.

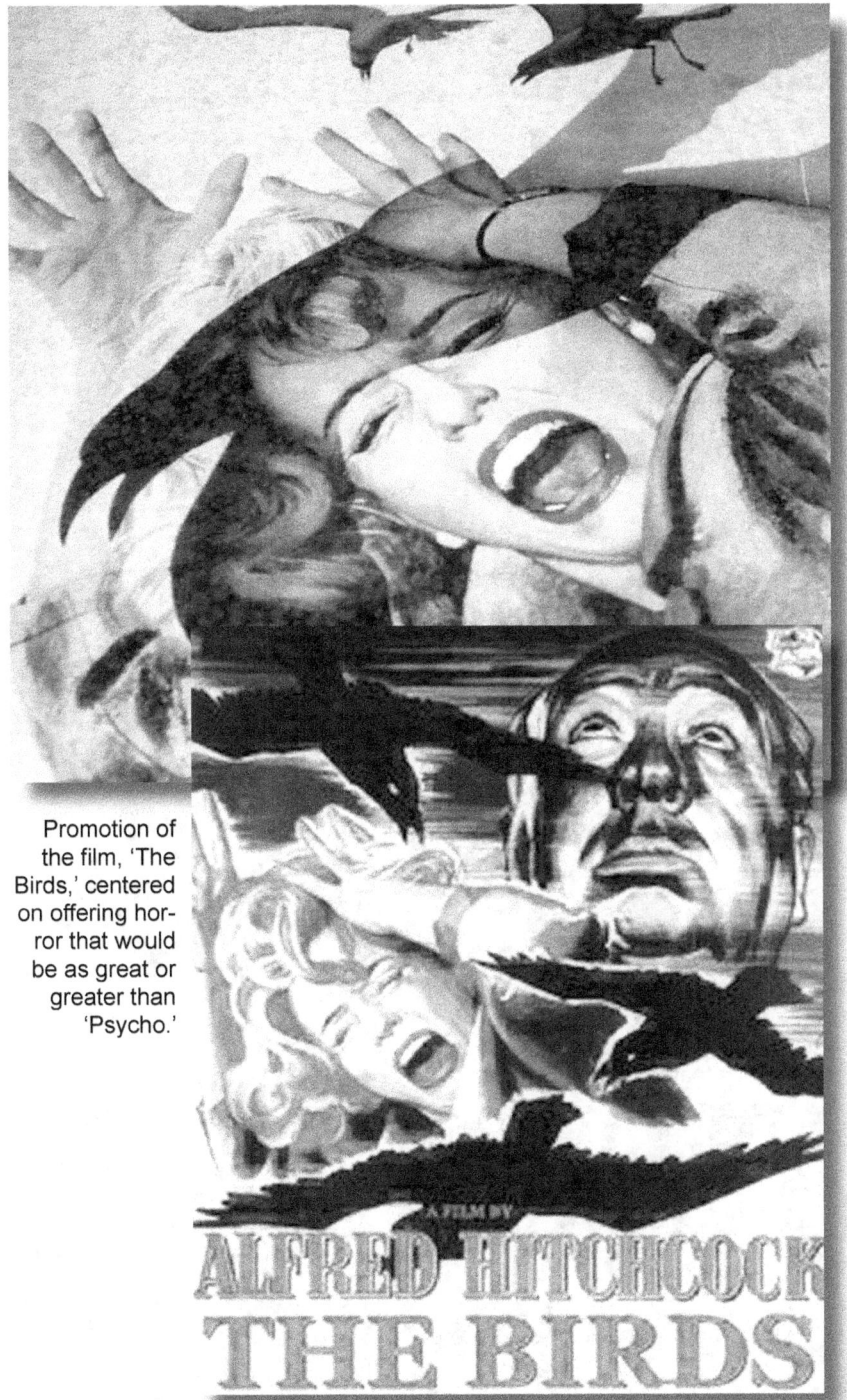

Promotion of the film, 'The Birds,' centered on offering horror that would be as great or greater than 'Psycho.'

ALFRED HITCHCOCK: the icon years

Bodega Bay, north of San Francisco, provided the backdrop for much of the action in 'The Birds.' Above, the church and below, Tides Wharf Restaurant were real locations featured in key scenes.

ALFRED HITCHCOCK: the icon years

In addition to films, TV and paperback books Hitchcock even lent his name and image to a board game that capitalized on his brand of suspense and mystery.

ALFRED HITCHCOCK: the icon years

Hitchcock would use his Hollywood birds to promote his 1963 horror.

ALFRED HITCHCOCK: the icon years

With smiles all around, Alfred Hitchcock accompanied Tippi Hedren to the Cannes Film Festival to present his 1963 film 'The Birds.' Hedren, as the leading lady of the film would already be gearing up for her second Hitchcock film, 'Marnie,' in 1964. And while she was at one time planning even a third film with the director to follow 'Marnie,' a falling out with the director would cause him to cancel the film and end his association with Hedren.

ALFRED HITCHCOCK: the icon years

Rod Taylor and Tippi Hedren were both relative newcomers to major motion pictures when Hitchcock cast them as lovers in 'The Birds.'

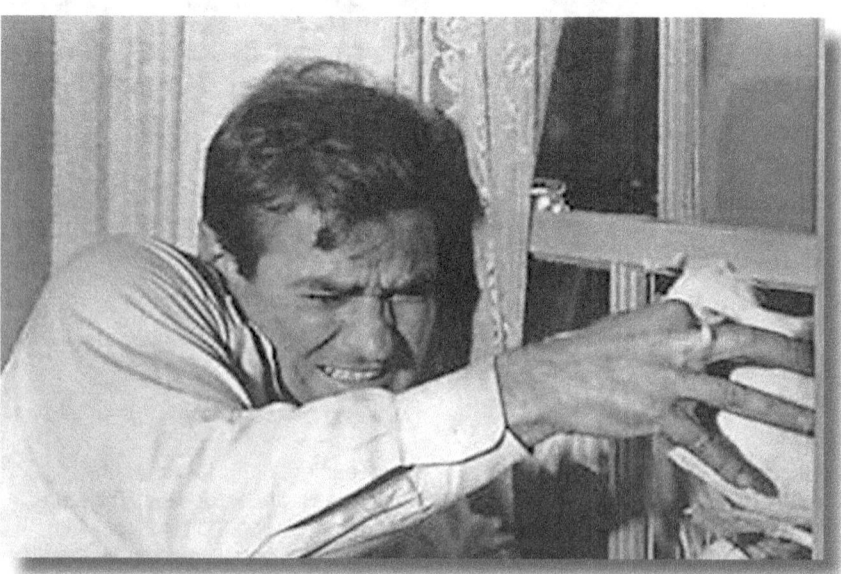

Rod Taylor fit the mold of the standard Hitchcock leading man. With rugged features like other Hitchcock actors, Cary Grant and John Gavin, Taylor's leading role in 'The Birds' had him acting as much with feathered co-stars as he did with human ones.

ALFRED HITCHCOCK: the icon years

Hitchcock has long been a favorite of film magazines. In addition to his own magazines, Hitchcock has frequented many magazine covers as journalists continue to analyze and discuss his work and its impact on film.

Promotion for 'Marnie.'

Tippi Hedren and Sean Connery in a scene from 'Marnie.'

Hitchcock again used his own likeness to promote 'Torn Curtain' instead of its stars Paul Newman and Julie Andrews.

ALFRED HITCHCOCK: the icon years

Hitchcock's most famous film location, the Bates Motel and infamous home of Norman Bates held residence on the Universal lot for many years and was recreated in Florida at Universal Studios theme park. The various locations have been used over the years for several sequels, including 'Psycho II' and 'Psycho III' as well as the cable prequel 'Psycho IV.'

Hitchcock's TV series would end in the mid-1960s after nearly 10 years on the small screen, but it would make him one of the most recognizable faces and richest men in Hollywood.

Hitchcock would use his name and face to promote everything from films, TV shows, books, a fan magazine, board games and even music albums.

ALFRED HITCHCOCK: the icon years

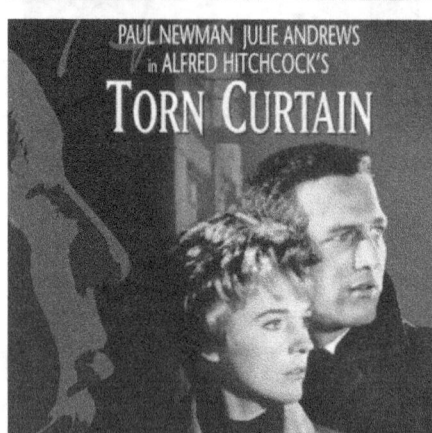

Universal DVD releases of Hitchcock's films continue find audiences as films are re-issued with extra features and new digital transfers of the original films.

ALFRED HITCHCOCK: the icon years

Universal was wise to promote their association with Hitchcock and his long career in the film industry. His PR photos during his later years used his many successes and numerous films to remind viewers that Hitchcock's newest film 'Family Plot' would be the latest in the long line of suspense hits.

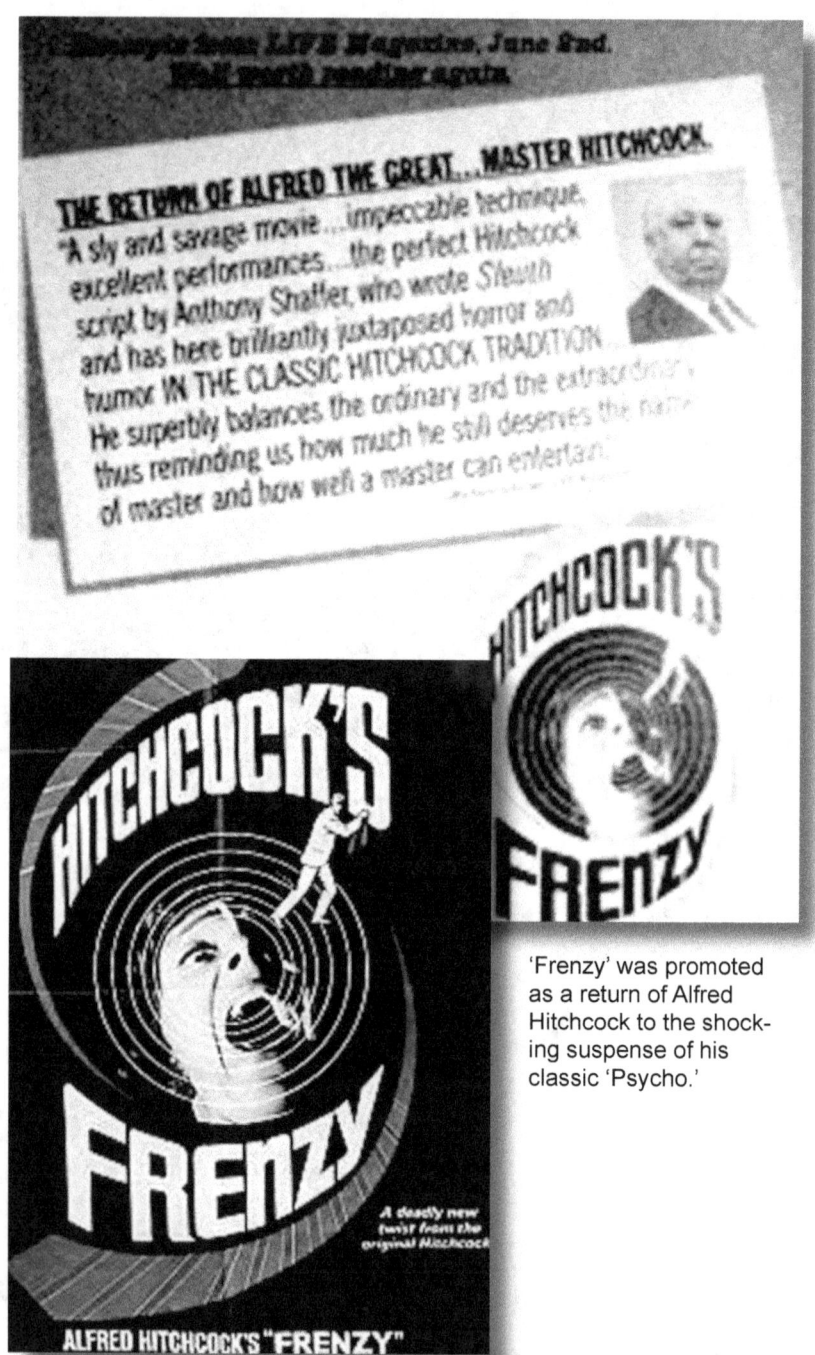

'Frenzy' was promoted as a return of Alfred Hitchcock to the shocking suspense of his classic 'Psycho.'

ALFRED HITCHCOCK: the icon years

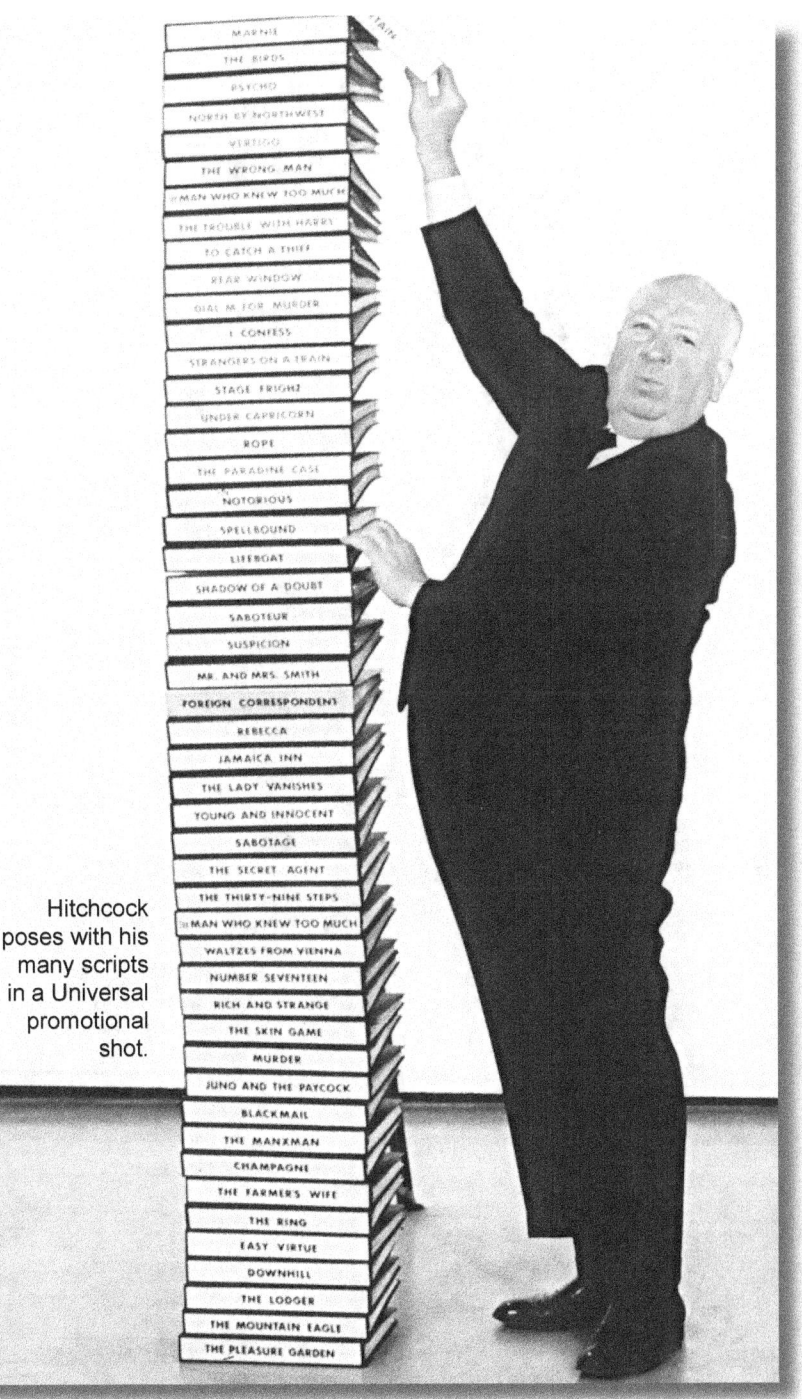

Hitchcock poses with his many scripts in a Universal promotional shot.

ALFRED HITCHCOCK: the icon years

Hitchcock, true to form, would again use himself as a marketing point to promote his final film, 'Family Plot' when it was released in March 1976.

ALFRED HITCHCOCK: the icon years

eleven

ALFRED HITCHCOCK: the icon years

ALFRED HITCHCOCK: the icon years

"In films murders are always very clean. I show how difficult it is and what a messy thing it is to kill a man."

Alfred Hitchcock

Torn Curtain

All the elements, but still not topping expectations for Hitchcock's 1966 thriller

Julie Andrews was riding high in 1965. Not only was she embarking on a romance with her soon-to-be-husband Blake Edwards, but she was also about to star in one of the most successful motion pictures of all time, *The Sound of Music*. And if that wasn't good enough, that spring she was named Best Actress by the Academy of Motion Pictures Arts and Sciences at its annual Oscar ceremony for her performance in *Mary Poppins*.

ALFRED HITCHCOCK: the icon years

Interestingly enough, it was two days before the Oscar awards that she first met with Alfred Hitchcock to discuss a starring role in his next picture. Like most actors she was eager to work with the director and agreed. She was good box office draw and Universal forced her on Hitchcock. Reluctant as he was Hitchcock didn't have the clout to reject a star of the caliber of Julie Andrews.

The reality was that in January 1966, months before the release of *Torn Curtain*, Quigley's *Motion Picture Herald* released the results of its annual survey of United States cinema exhibitors and Julie Andrews was named the fourth biggest money-making draw on the big screen. She held company alongside Sean Connery, John Wayne and Doris Day. *The Sound of Music* was still breaking box office records.

Hitchcock himself was reluctant, saying "The audience will be waiting for her to sing." He also felt that while she was in many ways a cool and beautiful woman she was "more suited to the drawing room rather than the bedroom." She, on the other hand was eager for the chance to finally play a modern woman. *Torn Curtain* would offer her the first chance to play a contemporary character in modern times with equally modern morals. In fact, the opening sequence of the film features she and her co-star, an unmarried couple, in bed together. It was certainly a different side of Julie Andrews.

Some reports suggest that Hitchcock wanted to offer the leading lady role to Eva Marie Saint who he had successfully directed in *North By Northwest*, but Universal was set on Andrews. And for the leading man role Hitchcock was rumored to have suggested bringing Cary Grant back.

The Leading Man

But Julie Andrews was just half of Hitchcock's problems with the casting of *Torn Curtain*. Once again, the front office at Universal had their hooks into Hitchcock when they demanded he cast an equally big name star to the leading male role in the film. While Paul Newman fit the bill in many ways, he and Hitchcock never actually hit it off, but Universal's head office wanted him and Hitchcock gave in.

Hitchcock, to put it mildly, was "disenchanted" with Paul Newman. When Newman was invited to Hitchcock's home to discuss his starring role in the feature the story goes that he insulted the director by preferring to grab a can of beer from the refrigerator rather than sample the featured wine Hitchcock had selected for the dinner. The working style of the two men was also different and Paul Newman didn't have the same style and taste of a Cary Grant and Hitchcock never quite took to him. Newman also had a background as a method actor and Hitchcock wasn't really concerned with motivation behind his character, he only cared about how he moved before his camera. The two styles clashed.

Julie Andrews on the other hand had a fondness for Paul Newman. She didn't know him well, but had been introduced to him at a social gathering several years earlier and recalled it well. It was at a party in 1963 when another guest brought the pair together. The guest said something along the lines of, "Do you know Julie Andrews," to begin the introduction when Newman responded, "Of course I know Julie Andrews. "She's the last of the really great broads."

"Nobody has ever called me that," replied Andrews with a smile and a laugh. "I wouldn't mind having that as my epitaph."

While Newman didn't have the current star power Julie Andrews did he was about to come out with *Harper*, one of his more successful ventures of the 60s. And *Cool Hand Luke*, released a year after *Torn Curtain* would help further his superstar status.

So, with his stars in place Hitchcock was free to begin putting the pieces of his *Torn Curtain* together. While he was not at all convinced the pairing would offer the chemistry he desired, there was little he could do about it. Hitchcock was no longer free to disband with the demands of the production office. By the latter part of the 60s he had once again begun to falter. With the miserable box office performance of *Marnie* as well as his own lack of interest in the film by the time it was ready for release gave Universal reason for concern. And when his television show, *Alfred Hitchcock Presents*, was canceled during the 1964-65 TV season his work was now fraught with risk. Not only were his films expensive to make, but the promotion of them was also key. His own persona was intrinsically tied to each release and if his name became associated with failure or mediocrity, it endangered the potential for each subsequent release.

The one drawback of big name stars was the cost. Hitchcock often preferred to keep stars out of the way or at a low cost, but with the pair, the studio paid about $1.8 million dollars for the lead actors. Julie Andrews in fact was at a higher salary than Newman because her stardom was at its peak, but her role by the time the script was ready was less than spectacular.

Based on a True Story

The tale was originally based on a true story that Hitchcock had been fascinated with for years. Guy Burgess and Donald MacLean were British diplomats who acted as double agents for the Soviet Union in the late 1940s while high up in the British government. By 1951, while they were being investigated for their actions, the pair defected and fled to Russia.

It was a story that Hitchcock thought would make a thrilling suspense film. The adventure and international intrigue was paired with danger and tales of infidelity, homosexuality and betrayal. It had a lot of layers Hitchcock felt would be interesting to explore. He felt the central theme would focus on a struggle of love or duty.

In 1965, looking for his next project, Hitch dusted off the old idea and decided to see if there was life still in the story. He knew he needed a top writer to help craft the tale into a first-rate screenplay, but after his first writing choice was tied to another project and unavailable, he got a recommendation from a story editor at Universal who suggested he talk to a writer by the name of Brian Moore. Moore was mostly interested in writing novels, but to pay the bills he was sometimes willing to turn his talents to other endeavors.

Moore met with Hitchcock and initially felt it would be a great opportunity to work with someone as successful and interesting as Alfred Hitchcock. However, after hearing the director's ideas Moore didn't think he was right for the project. A few days later, after thinking it over, Moore turned down Hitchcock's offer, much to the director's surprise. But Hitchcock wasn't about to give up so easily. He doubled his offer from $25,000 to $50,000 and the lure of the large payout caused Moore to change his mind. "I arrived very much against my own judgment," recalled Moore. "But willing to do the best I could."

A Movie Takes Shape

Moore met with Hitchcock daily at his Universal offices through the summer of 1965 as the story was fleshed out. But with Julie Andrews and Paul Newman signed on to star the references to homosexuality were thrown out as impossible as Universal would never allow it. The budget was set at $5 million, but roughly $2 million went to acting salaries, so far off location shooting had to be clipped and the film would be made entirely on the Universal lot with on some second unit footage shot for backdrops and rear projection footage.

Through the fall the screenplay was fleshed out and a script produced. The film's name was finally settled – *Torn Curtain*. And while Moore found the experience an interesting one, by the time the script was done he realized he had actually contributed very little of his own ideas to the story. Most of it was chronicling a concept driven by Hitchcock. Moore recalled that he only had three original ideas of his own that would make it into the final film.

Moore's suggestion that the entire premise center around a scientist's need for information from another scientist's head – a formula – that he must coax out of a Communist scientist was the first contribution. A second idea from Moore was a small side story where a woman allies herself to the scientist and his wife in order to gain sponsor so she could defect to the West. His final idea suggestion surrounded the demise of a Russian agent. Moore felt movies always made murder and death look too easy. But he believed it was actually an ugly and difficult situation and that it didn't always happen quite as simply as movie writers often depicted. So he helped craft a graphic murder sequence in which the victim is stabbed, beaten, wrestled to the ground, dragged across the floor and gassed to death with his head forced into an oven. All the while, his arms, legs and hands twitching and struggling as his killers hold him in place until he perishes. It would be one of the most graphic murder sequences on film from Hitchcock.

Hitchcock considered setting the story in Poland but later opted for East Berlin. Before the filming began he actually traveled on vacation to places where key scenes of the story take place, including Copenhagen and East Berlin.

The Troubled Script

When Julie Andrews received the final script she was saddened to find the woman's perspective she had been promised was all but gone from the feature. While her role was that of an assistant to a nuclear physicist where she spends most of her time pining after or puzzled by her scientist fiancé as he defects to the Soviet Union to obtain a secret formula. She had silly lines like "East Berlin? But, but, that's behind the iron curtain!"

Her future husband cannot include her in his treachery because he doesn't want to put her in danger because he's actually only using the defection as a trick to get to the Russian scientist. But she defects along with him much to his surprise. She then has very little to do but follow him around as he tries to get the life-threatening formula and escape the country. With his would-be wife in tow he then makes a daring escape after he's got what he needs. One story suggests that at one point Hitchcock considered changing the ending of the film and had Newman throwing away the secret formula to keep everyone from getting the secret, but it was felt that after all the drama of the story, moviegoers would be disappointed that it was all for nothing.

The script was mainly complete but needed some additional work so Hitchcock hired another set of writers to help bring things together and punch up the dialogue. Moore had given all he could to the project and eventually told Hitchcock he thought the screenplay was weak and that the characters were somewhat unbelievable. He even said, "If it were a book I was writing – I'd scrap it or do a complete rewrite."

Finishing the Film

Hitchcock was insulted and decided he was done with Moore. He hired the new writers and stopped discussing the film with Moore. Moore offered to have his name taken off the film, but Hitchcock refused.

When the new writers wanted equal screen credit for the screenplay the situation grew more dramatic and the case was submitted to the Screen Writers Guild for arbitration, eventually finding in favor of Moore as the official screenwriter.

Julie Andrews tried her best to remain enthusiastic and remembered Hitchcock as funny, possessive and endearing. "I accepted for the chance to work with Hitchcock," she recalled. "And he taught me more about film and lenses than anyone. It was a wonderful education, but he was obviously more interested in manipulating people, and in getting a reaction from the audience, than he was in directing us."

Andrews also had a common response after Hitch greeted members of the cast and crew by saying that the fun part of the project was over for him once he had worked out all the details. "You can imagine how that made us feel," she told one Hitchcock biographer.

Paul Newman wasn't as kind of the working experience or the film. He actually sent Hitchcock a letter spelling out many of his concerns while the film was in production. He always felt that had the script been better he and Hitchcock might have gotten along much better. Newman liked the idea after Hitchcock had originally described the story, but was disappointed with the resulting script. "... all during shooting we all wished we didn't have to make it," Newman said. "The only good thing was we didn't have any location work, since all the European settings were built right there on the Universal lot."

As pre-production was in high gear, the new writers were still working out scenes and script elements and things were still not complete when filming began. According to writer Keith Waterhouse "... we found ourselves revising scenes only hours before they were to be shot."

The director had his own misgivings as well, but he centered his frustration on his casting problems and never considered the story might be part of the issue. "We'd have done much better with that picture without Julie Andrews or Paul Newman. Bad chemistry, that was." Hitchcock told one interviewer.

But dressed in one of his multiple identical blue suits, a starched white shirt and simple tie, he struggled through each day of what he found to be an unhappy production. He was lifted by a visit to the set from Britain's Princess Margaret and Lord Snowden in November 1965 during a trip to the United States. The famous royal couple looked forward to a chance to chat with the UK's most famous director and its biggest female star.

Much of the production felt rushed for the director. The script suffered and didn't reportedly receive enough development because Julie Andrews had only a short window of opportunity to complete the film, so Hitch had to utilize her while he had her and had to move ahead regardless of the state of the script. In fact, after Newman suffered serious injuries in a motorcycle crash required filming didn't allow him much time to heal and in early scenes he is featured with a raincoat over his arm to hide his injury.

One of the first scenes Newman and Andrews filmed together was the opening sequence of them, an unmarried couple, in bed together. The script had them huddled under the sheets and blankets making love and keeping warm as the temperature was freezing outside.

However, in reality it was what some recalled as "boiling hot" at the time of the filming. There were fans being blown under the blankets on the set to keep the stars cool, but Julie Andrews recalled they felt more like "slithering" away from the scene rather than the "shivering" the script called for.

Hitchcock placed his own cameo fairly early on in the film, a common thing for him to do in later years. In *Torn Curtain* he sitting in a hotel lobby bouncing a baby on one knee and then the other as the actors pass by.

Hitch liked getting the tradition of his cameo appearances out of the way early on. With his popularity, he found that filmgoers would be distracted from the story if they spent too much time looking for him to show up, so he ended that suspense early by inserting himself into his later movies usually within the first few scenes.

The Finished Product

By February 1966 filming was completed, but the budget had spiraled to $6 million and cast and crew still didn't think the added expense had helped. Paul Newman summed it up best by telling writer Donald Spoto, "We all knew we had a loser on our hands in this picture."

All in all, *Torn Curtain* wasn't the failure some had predicted. The film grossed some $6.5 million in the U.S. alone thereby making back its cost and then some before moving into worldwide release. It hit theaters in the U.S. in July 1966 and found a U.K. release at the same time, but later releases in Sweden, Japan, West Germany, Spain, France, Finland and Denmark would help bring in additional profits to Universal. Some reports put the film's total box office take at $13 million.

Review Are In

Variety called it "an OK cold war suspenser," while *The New York Times* wasn't as kind in their review, calling it "a pathetically undistinguished spy picture."

While some, like *Life* magazine, focused on the failings of the script by writing it "lacks that constant crackle of smart dialogue that one usually associates with a Hitchcock enterprise," other critics discussed the failings of the performances. "Newman simply doesn't add up as a nuclear physicist," wrote the *New York Post*. "Maybe he was *Harper* too recently and was too good in it. And Julie Andrews doesn't resemble in any way the assistant to a nuclear physicist. She has been too much the Baroness and *Mary Poppins* or even Americanized Emily, to fit this chore."

But while some criticized the casting, as had Hitchcock, others came to the defense of the stars. *Variety* said "Newman gives a good underplaying to his role, while Miss Andrews' charming voice and appearance lend grace to a limited but billed-over-title role.

Hitchcock didn't come away unscathed by reviewers either. While many agreed that he was a legend, the title in itself left people expecting something more than what they got. *The New York Times* said "In these times, with James Bond capers and pallid spies coming in out of the cold, Mr. Hitchcock will have to give us something a good bit brighter to keep us amused."

Overall, *Torn Curtain* in some ways was a throw-back to Hitchcock's traditional filmmaking process. Shooting on a soundstage allowed him the control he desired, but filmmaking was taking a step forward and younger filmmakers were taking risks that put them outside the traditions and their work was being noticed for it. Hitchcock's work became visibly more dated and his approach would require updating.

In fact, several of the scenes in *Torn Curtain* capture scenes reminiscent of his previous work. The opening sequence features a soft-focus close-up kiss that was similar to shots Hitch included successfully in both *Rear Window* and *Marnie*. And the farmhouse sequences offers a very similar feel to *North By Northwest* when Cary Grant is walking across the opens spaces just prior to the crop-duster scenes. It features a "danger comes in the most ordinary places" approach.

In another scene, when Paul Newman at last lets Julie Andrews in on the secret the scene take place on a hillside that mirrors a similar scene between Rod Taylor and Tippi Hedren just prior to an attack in *The Birds*.

One scene Hitchcock left out would have been a flash back to *Vertigo* when, after killing the German agent in the farmhouse Paul Newman's character comes face to face with him again when he sees the man's look-a-like brother, who is holding a knife similar to the one that helped kill his brother. Hitch dropped the scene feeling it didn't add anything to progress the story.

After Effects

Hitchcock would rebound from *Torn Curtain*, as would all the major players. The film was by no means a colossal failure. The profits came in and the critics were not nearly as harsh on the film as they were on several other Hitchcock pictures.

While Hitchcock would take a break from filmmaking and Hollywood in 1967 he would return to the world he loved in 1968 with a new project and another attempt to once again wow the critics.

As for the stars, both Julie Andrews and Paul Newman would have the film be merely a bookmark in the larger tale of their careers. Both would make countless other films for many, many years. Some of those films were praised and found fans at the box office. Others, however, for both stars were less than spectacular. In fact, some fared far worse than *Torn Curtain*.

Another Unfinished Concept

But *Torn Curtain* wasn't the only project Hitchcock was working on at the time. He also was considering a film called *R.R.R.R.*, which was as much a caper as it was a suspense thriller.

The name *R.R.R.R.* comes from the letter "R" when used as a symbol for describing a rare coin. R.R. is very rare and R.R.R. is extremely rare. R.R.R.R. signals the top most rare value that can be placed on a coin and the story was based on an original idea of Hitchcock's. The story involves a New York City hotel that is run by an Italian immigrant and his family. But unbeknownst to the man, the hotel is being used as cover for criminal activity. And when a valuable coin is stolen from a guest of the hotel, drama, suspense and some comedy ensue.

Hitch hired a pair of Italian comedy-thriller writers, Agenore Incrocci and Furio Scarpelli, to help build on the idea. He liked their work on *Big Deal on Madonna Street*, and felt many Italian films at the time were ahead of his in style and pace. However language barriers between the screenwriters and director caused the project to languish. And when Universal didn't respond favorably to the idea, Hitchcock dropped the project.

ALFRED HITCHCOCK: the icon years

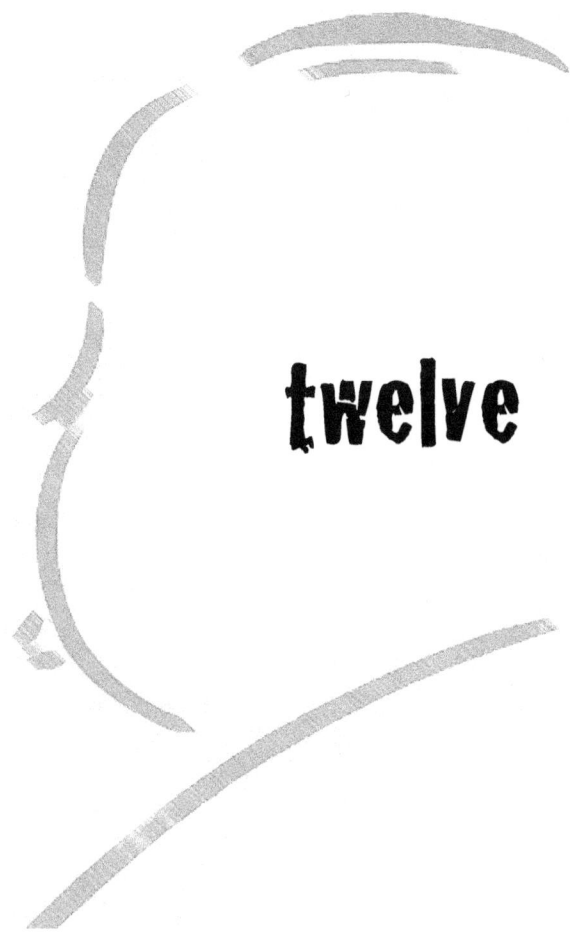

twelve

ALFRED HITCHCOCK: the icon years

ALFRED HITCHCOCK: the icon years

"If it's a good movie, the sound could go off and the audience would still have a perfectly clear idea of what was going on."
Alfred Hitchcock

The Auteur Filmmaker

Acclaim for a magnificent career and thoughts of a legacy

With *Torn Curtain* completed by the spring of 1966, all that was left was the arduous task of finalizing the promotion and dealing with all the media activities it took to get a movie to the public. While part of Hitchcock certainly hated the task of "selling" a movie there was a part of him driven by the adulation that accompanied a release.

For Hitchcock it was a struggle he would endure for his entire career. On the one hand once a film was completed in his head and story-boarded out he lost interest in anything that followed. He seemed bored by the camera work as well as the actors and frustrated when scripts were incomplete when production began. His stars often complained that Hitchcock failed to ever provide them any useful direction or motivation on the set. His main concern was to capture the actions and the angles he so desired and as long as the actors got their lines right and moved on cue to the rhythm he had demanded of them he was satisfied. While a few actors invited the freedom this provided, others struggled with it.

A Challenge for Actors

Actors like Gary Grant, Ingrid Bergman and Janet Leigh found working with Hitchcock a pleasure because they had the ability to define the internal make-up of the character and understood the constraints of what Hitchcock expected of them. While other actors, including his most recent experience with Paul Newman and Julie Andrews, seemed to require more dialogue and understanding of what they were expected to deliver and wanted more than a cue of where to walk or how to look.

But while Hitchcock bored of much of the filmmaking process that followed his screenplay, he adored the attention moviemaking offered him. For a portly, older fellow he longed for attention and found that being the "star" director had its pluses because he would be sought after and treated as a celebrity.

In fact, his TV series had turned him into more than just a household name – he had already been that – but by the sixties he was one of the most recognizable faces in Hollywood. And his desire for attention and acclaim was fueled by the release of each film. It gave him and opportunity to film TV spots, movie promotions, and plan advertising campaigns that centered on his likeness.

He gave interviews to TV, magazines and newspapers and loved the acclaim that came with each release. But if a movie was panned by critics he could suffer the agony of failure.

Honors from Home and Abroad

Before *Torn Curtain* would garner such reviews Hitch accepted an invitation to deliver an address at Cambridge. He accepted it for several reasons. First, it was a chance to head back to England. He always enjoyed traveling back to his homeland and any trip where he could tie it to his work was a welcome one. Second, he once again loved the notoriety of being sought after as a speaker. For others to want to hear what he had to say was what drove him to do what he did.

So, that summer, in June he flew to the United Kingdom to address to the Cambridge University Film Society. The event offered both a chance for Hitchcock to deliver an address and then take part in a discussion period with the students about his work. When asked about the future of film he told the audience, "Mass hypnotism would be a nice idea for the future. You buy a ticket and choose the character you want to be," said Hitchcock. "If you want to be the villain, then you have a good time being the villain. If you want to be the tortured victim, you can suffer."

Hitch then continued to bask in the glory of his long and successful career by accepting New York City's Cultural Medal of Honor in July. He flew from London to New York for a ceremony at City Hall where the honor was bestowed upon him. He also gave a series of media interviews and the event provided him an opportunity to also tout his upcoming release before the reviews would come in.

His summer of adulation continued when he headed to Massachusetts to accept an honor from then Governor John Volpe when the governor declared July 14, 1966 as Alfred Hitchcock Day across the Commonwealth of Massachusetts. Then it was off to Boston University for another special citation for his career accomplishments. And the to top things off Harvard University also gave him an honorary membership to the Harvard Drama Club that month.

Also in July Hitchcock was invited to Toronto to address the students of the University of Toronto on "The Art and Business of Filmmaking." He also spoke to The Directors Guild of Canada and then it was back to London where he was honored with an award from the Association of Cinematograph, Television and Allied Technicians. He then attended a luncheon in London that August where the London Film Society and others forgave Hitchcock for abandoning his homeland and the work of European filmmaking for Hollywood. The association then hosted a dinner where Hitchcock was awarded an honorary membership.

Hitchcock returned to his Los Angeles home at the end of the summer and even though the reviews of his latest work were less than enthusiastic he was warmed by the acclaim he had earned by his complete body of work and one film wouldn't detract from all that he had accomplished.

Back in Hollywood

Also in 1967 the Academy of Motion Picture Arts and Sciences would honor Hitchcock at their annual Academy Awards ceremony with the coveted Irving Thalberg award for his contribution to cinema. The academy presented him with the award saying, "When you examine the list of his films you are jolted by the legion of absolutely top level entertainment he has made – a record almost unmatched by any director practicing his magic anywhere ... a body of work so distinctive that his name has passed into the language ... his briefly titled masterpieces of suspense, adventure and humor have endeared him to film buffs as certainly as his own fey presence on the small screen has endeared him to television audiences."

By the end of August fellow filmmaker Francois Truffaut was welcomed by Hitchcock for a series of interviews. In fact, in one of the most detailed efforts chronicling Hitchcock's views, Truffaut recorded more than 50 hours of discussion between himself and the master of suspense as Hitchcock discussed his films, actors and career in great length and much detail. The recordings would result in both book and audio releases and offer film historians one of the most comprehensive looks at the career of Alfred Hitchcock by the director himself. It would also further cement his icon status in the world of film.

But even an icon didn't have free reign in Hollywood - certainly not at Universal. Hitchcock had come up with an idea for a new film about a psychopathic homosexual killer who was the son of a respected general. He hired a writer and crafted a screenplay, but Universal rejected the script, thinking it was too far outside the mainstream of what audiences expected from Hitchcock.

Hitchcock, reportedly, was so disappointed in their response that he nearly burst into tears. He then became so jaded by Universal and the world of Hollywood that he receded from the world of filmmaking. He would be virtually unseen for all of 1967. Some began to wonder if he would ever be back to make a new film.

ALFRED HITCHCOCK: the icon years

ALFRED HITCHCOCK: the icon years

thirteen

ALFRED HITCHCOCK: the icon years

ALFRED HITCHCOCK: the icon years

"Dialogue should simply be a sound among other sounds, just something that comes out of the mouths of people whose eyes tell the story in visual terms."

Alfred Hitchcock

Topaz

The film fails to reach expectations but gives fans another Hitchcock classic to discuss

After a hiatus in 1967 Hitchcock was anxious to get back to work by 1968. In reality it was in part his wife Alma who pushed him to it. His despondence over the failures of his last few films, including his inability get *Mary Rose* to the screen, as well as his difficulty in finding a suitable story that would satisfy both him and Universal left him stagnant. But in the early part of 1968 he finally selected a project and began preparing to once again direct.

Topaz was a novel by Leon Uris. Uris was an American novelist whose first novel, *Battle Cry,* was published in 1953. But his claim to fame wouldn't come until about five years later when *Exodus,* his third novel, became a best seller. After the book was translated into more than a dozen languages it was turned into a feature film in 1960 starring Paul Newman. *Topaz* became his latest best seller after its release in 1967 and Universal quickly purchased the film rights that fall.

A Tale of Espionage

The story behind *Topaz* is based in part on a factual tale from 1962 during the Cuban Missile Crisis. It is an epic tale where the French, the Americans, the Russians, and the Cubans are embroiled in a dirty exchange of government secrets and lies. While the book and subsequent film had a wide collection of characters, international locales and drama, it was a bit short on the usual elements of suspense that made Hitchcock's films work and it certainly lacked the horrific elements that had made the only hits of the director's recent series of films. In fact, *Topaz* in some ways resembled more the elements of *Torn Curtain* that failed to capture the imagination of moviegoers for Hitchcock's last outing.

However, under contact to Universal to deliver a film and without anything else on the horizon Hitchcock decided the project would be a suitable one. The director described the feature as "The story of espionage in high places," while later marketing of the film would promote the film by saying "Hitchcock takes you behind the actual headlines to expose the most explosive spy scandal of the century!"

The title, *Topaz,* comes from a code name for a Russian spy ring within the French government in Uris' novel. Uris was contracted by Universal to deliver the first draft of the screenplay to the studio and Hitchcock hired Herbert Coleman as his associate producer. Hitchcock then set forth on scouting locations for the production. He also had to find suitable actors for the key roles. It was initially suggested that Yves Montand and Catherine Deneuve might make suitable stars, but Hitchcock rejected the idea.

Hitch had been stung before by big name stars distracting his production and costing money he felt could be better spent on other aspects of a film. Perhaps his recent experience with Paul Newman and Julie Andrews being forced upon his *Torn Curtain* soured the idea. The director selected lesser known actors, Frederick Stafford and Dany Robbin as his leading French characters in the feature and Claude Jade was cast as their daughter.

Stafford, according to some of the promotional materials for the film was most notable for having been considered as a replacement for Sean Connery in the James Bond series, but he turned the role down. Universal was keen to promote any association with the Bond franchise, which was very successful at the time.

For the most part, few of the actors had any notoriety with American film audiences though, but Hitchcock did employ John Forsythe in a key role as an American agent embroiled in the espionage. Forsythe was familiar, but not a major star. He had worked heavily in television and also worked with Hitchcock before in *The Trouble with Harry*. Karin Dor was offered a key role as a Cuban heroine involved in an affair with Stafford's character, but it was a last minute casting after many others had been considered. The rest of the cast included competent actors but no stars to outshine the director.

Troubled Film

Even so, Hitchcock found the entire production of *Topaz* a troubling one. The script that came forth from Uris was considered unusable by Hitchcock's standards. And he had difficulty in obtaining anyone to provide a suitable rewrite. As production began the director still didn't have a script to shoot with.

The story goes that he called his old friend Samuel Taylor for help. Taylor, who had turned *Sabrina* into a hit and had helped Hitchcock roughly a decade earlier on *Vertigo* came to the director's rescue and provided the necessary rewrites to get him through the production. Taylor claimed that Hitchcock basically tossed out the entire Uris script and had him writing and re-writing scenes just hours before they were filmed. It was a difficult set of circumstances for everyone involved. Taylor struggled to keep pace with the production and actors were being given lines and scenes with little time for preparation. And for a director who commonly worked out all the elements, scenes and shots in his head months before a production began, it was a sad state of affairs and gave Universal reason for concern.

The film would become Hitchcock's most expensive picture to date and problems carried through to the end of the production when Hitchcock couldn't find an appropriate conclusion to the tale. He actually filmed a series of different endings and the studio put its final approvals on how the film would end, even when selecting an ending that was contrary to what the director wished. One ending included a duel and an assassination while another had the characters departing on separate planes. In total, three different endings were shot. " One of the tragedies of *Topaz*," recalled screenwriter Samuel Taylor, "was that Hitch was trying to make something as if he had Ingrid Bergman and Cary Grant. But he didn't have the story for it and he certainly didn't have the cast."

A Less than Spectacular Release

The critics were perhaps kinder to the film than the director was. Hitchcock said *Topaz* was "a most unhappy picture to make." *The New York Times* wrote that the film "is not a conventional Hitchcock film. It's rather too leisurely and the machinations of plot rather too convoluted to be easily summed up in anything except a very loose sentence." But they also called the film "pure Hitchcock, a movie of beautifully composed sequences, full of surface tensions, ironies, absurdities ..."

But not all the reviews offered praise. Some said the "plot failed to gather momentum" and that the cast was not a particularly memorable one. Pauline Kael perhaps was one of the harshest critics, wrote "The embarrassment of *Topaz* is that Hitchcock is lazy and out of touch."

The U.S. domestic box office figures vary with estimates putting the take at roughly $3 million. Some moviegoers were put off by the length of the movie because it clocked in at nearly two-and-a-half hours. Even so, some reports put the film's worldwide box office take in excess of $6 million.

To promote the worldwide release Hitchcock embarked on massive promotional tour, in part, because Universal felt the film would need all the help it could get. At 70 years old, Hitchcock used every bit of stamina he had to tour some 50 cities, giving more than 100 press interviews, and visiting 21 radio shows and appeared in more than 90 television talk shows.

If the film succeeded at all it was in that several of his previous releases, including *Marnie* and *Torn Curtain* were singled out by critics as dated by their use of rear projection of showing location footage on a screen in the background instead of actually shooting on location. It was a style Hitchcock was comfortable with because it allowed him control over lighting, sound and other elements, but modern filmmakers began using it less in an effort to capture more realism by the camera. In *Topaz* Hitchcock was credited with having caught up to more current filmmakers. "*Topaz* dazzles with location photography in Paris, Copenhagen, and New York, and meticulously recreated sets in Hollywood," one writer noted.

It wasn't the perfect way to end the decade, but the film fared much better than some expected. And once again, Hitchcock's status as an icon enabled him to move past *Topaz* somewhat unscathed as he still carried the title master of suspense.

ALFRED HITCHCOCK: the icon years

ALFRED HITCHCOCK: the icon years

fourteen

ALFRED HITCHCOCK: the icon years

ALFRED HITCHCOCK: the icon years

"Drama is life with the dull bits cut out."

Alfred Hitchcock

Accolades & Honors

An impressive body of work is honored

While *Topaz* was in process Hitchcock received a personal boost during what he considered a very difficult production when the University of California at Santa Cruz gave him an honorary doctorate for his accomplishments in the world of cinema. It was a welcome opportunity to once again bask in the glow of adoration and accept the acclaim as an icon dedicated to the world of film by students looking at him as both a master and teacher.

Hitchcock had begun to find during the 60s that in addition to interviews from the press or radio and television programs he was sought after as an educator. The interest around his series of interviews with Francois Truffaut, coupled with the frequent invitations to universities for honorary awards, certificates and degrees meant that at last he was being respected not only as a successful filmmaker, but as a talented and artistic one.

Teaching Young Filmmakers

The director would again be honored just before the release of his next film, *Frenzy*, when he accepted an honorary doctorate at Columbia University. And an advance print of the upcoming picture was provided to the University of Southern California at about the same time, so both coasts had the opportunity to celebrate and honor the director at major educational institutions. His art and insight were on full display.

Sandwiched between his films, in February 1970, Hitch took part in another opportunity to talk about his career and his body of work. He attended an American Film Institute event hosted by the Center for Advanced Film Studies where, before an audience of students, he spoke about his views on actors and theatergoers, as well on the differences between suspense, surprise, mystery and the thriller.

"There is a great confusion between the words 'mystery' and 'suspense'," Hitchcock explained to the students and budding filmmakers. "The two things are absolutely miles apart. Mystery in an intellectual process, like a whodunit. But suspense is essentially an emotional process."

For Hitchcock mystery held no allure for him. He was far more interested in the suspense that came with it. It was the emotional action and reaction and the need to predict and capture it that fascinated the master of suspense.

And as 1970 wore on he was looking at his next chance to capture it and give audiences what they had always wanted from a Hitchcock film – the ultimate in suspense.

While *Frenzy* would be that film, Hitchcock had tried to get a similar project off the ground several times, reportedly between 1964 and 1967, but without success.

A Different 'Frenzy'

A film that Hitchcock referred to at different times as either *Frenzy* or *Kaleidoscope*, originally was intended to be a prequel, of sorts, to *Shadow of a Doubt*, one of the director's clear successes of the 50s. Hitchcock reportedly approached numerous different writers about helping him flesh out the story, including Samuel Taylor and Ben Levy. Levy came closest to helping Hitch get his story into a usable script.

The story centered on a young, handsome bodybuilder who lures women to their death, much in the fashion of the "Merry Widow Murderer" from *Shadow of a Doubt*. The New York police set a trap by using a young policewoman as bait to trap the killer.

The script reportedly included three key suspense scenes created by the master of suspense that he mapped out in great detail as he had done with many murder sequences in previous films. One was a murder near a waterfall, and a second on an old warship. For the finale, Hitchcock planned to put the climactic attempted murder scene at an oil refinery.

Hitchcock with less restrictions from the censors intended to be much more blatant with the sex and violence. Where he was held back in *Psycho*, he felt audiences in the 1970s expected and could handle more. One 1967 version of the story had the murderer as a homosexual. Universal executives felt the tale was too much for Hitchcock audiences and refused to bankroll the film even though Hitch promised he could make the film for less than $1 million. He even worked out ideas on casting that included either, David Hemmings, Robert Redford, or Michael Caine in the lead.

But Hitchcock finally got his *Frenzy* made several years later, though the film would be quite different from the original one he had in mind.

ALFRED HITCHCOCK: the icon years

ALFRED HITCHCOCK: the icon years

fifteen

ALFRED HITCHCOCK: the icon years

ALFRED HITCHCOCK: the icon years

"As I do not approve of the current wave of violence that we see on our screens, I have always felt that murder should be treated delicately."

Alfred Hitchcock

Frenzy

The famous director returns to familiar territory and comes away with a big hit

It had been more than 20 years since Hitchcock shot a feature film in the United Kingdom. *Stage Fright* in 1950 was his last effort and the film didn't achieve the level of success the director had hoped for. But England was his native home and he traveled there often and Britain welcomed him back.

The London Times announced the news in January 1971, reporting, "He is in London until Thursday seeking locations for *Frenzy*, a thriller about a multiple murderer which will be filmed in April in and around London and in a British studio."

The newspaper even wrote he was staying at his favorite hotel Claridges and that he would be selecting a cast of all English actors for the film.

It would be his 52nd film and during the summer of 1970 he began the process of selecting the tale on which it would be based. The powers at Universal told Hitchcock in no uncertain terms that his over-budget and badly-cast feature with troubled script experience of *Topaz* could not be repeated. While he may have been an icon, they expected to approve the cast, the script and the costs if they were to fund and release another film. The director needed to accept their terms. As one of the largest shareholders Hitchcock also understood that the studio was in business to make money and that it wasn't entirely for artistic sake. If it had been any other director besides himself he would have expected the same treatment.

A Novel Idea

The idea he found came from the book *It Always Rains on Sunday* by Arthur La Bern. The tale is one of a London rapist and murderer and Hitchcock had read the novel before thinking it might make a proper thriller. He decided to once again to consider it. One of the reasons the story appealed to him was he thought he could do something special with the tale, inserting his own special flair on the suspense combined with elements of dark humor. He also thought he'd be able to make a first-rate thriller far cheaper and quicker in London than he could in Hollywood. And he would be right.

Casting a set of British actors would allow him a top notch group of talented performers who knew their way around the stage and movie set but it would also help keep costs down. It also would allow him to continue as the "star" of his own motion picture. And with qualified talent he could focus on getting the shots he needed without a lot of wasted effort. Universal agreed to Hitchcock's plan. The budget would be roughly $2 million.

He looked to the London theatre for the film's stars and cast Jon Finch, Barry Foster, Anna Massey, Vivien Merchant, Michael Bates and Alec McCowen in the key roles. He told the press he specifically went for character actors rather than stars "because this is a fairly realistic film and the audience knows that someone like Cary Grant can never be a murderer."

Hitchcock hired Anthony Shaffer to help him craft the novel into a usable screenplay and add depth to the characters. Shaffer had recently found success in London and New York with his play *Sleuth* and Shaffer thought it was a joke when Alfred Hitchcock called to say he wanted to work with him. It wasn't until he actually met the director that he realized it was no joke. The title was always intended to be *Frenzy*, regardless of what road the tale took. Perhaps he was trying to recapture the allure of *Psycho*. And he had the name in mind from a similar project several years earlier that never made it to production.

Hitchcock, with the help of Shaffer, worked on the story for months and the director described his next movie as "the story of a man who is impotent and therefore expresses himself through murder."

On Location

Location scouting in early 1971 proved successful when Hitchcock selected key locations in Covent Garden, Oxford Street, the Coburg Hotel, The Old Bailey Court and County Hall. And according to some, it was Shaffer who suggested Hitchcock include locations like the London Hilton and New Scotland Yard because they offered a more modern look at London that would complement the old London that Hitch was so fond of.

Director of Photography, Gil Taylor recalled that Hitchcock was very economical during the production, often "printing on the first take" because he knew exactly what he was looking for. He also fondly noted, "He is bigger than any star I have met."

Jon Finch, one of the film's leading men, said Hitchcock was visually strong but not as concerned when it came to the dialogue. It was a comment many actors would make after working with the director. "Some of the lines are frankly unbelievable, but he has told us to change anything we like," said Finch during the filming, "so all the actors are getting together to work out something reasonable."

Co-star Barry Foster, found working with Hitchcock a pleasure. "Before I met him. I expected Mr. Hitchcock to be a rather intimidating personality," he recalled. "In fact he is a very kind man and will do anything to help you. He exudes the feeling that nothing of this is crucial and it can be done again, which has an enormously relaxing effect on the actor."

Hitchcock was also very pleased with the production and the actors. He reportedly told his friend Samuel Taylor, "It's so wonderful to be back here! I'd forgotten what actors could do for me. They're not only prepared, they have ideas of their own – marvelous little bits of business."

A Graphic Murder

The most dramatic scene was that of the rape and murder of Barbara Leigh-Hunt. It was shot over a period of three days and was similar to *Psycho*'s shower scene murder of Janet Leigh in that it was broken up into a series of graphic shots and angles. The infamous necktie for the strangulation was actually sewn in the middle so that the tie could be pulled on from both ends as dramatically as possible without endangering the actress. The scene was far more graphic than anything Hitch had ever done before. Hitchcock was most pleased with the way things were rolling along.

But Hitchcock's excitement and interest in the film would change midway through production when his wife Alma suffered a stroke. The event came quite suddenly and surprised the director. Partially paralyzed and having difficulty with her speech, Alma was at first stabilized in London and then transported back to their home in Los Angeles where she could be treated in the comforts of her own home and by doctors and staff who she felt more comfortable with.

Hitchcock was required to struggle on without her for the remaining weeks of filming. It was both a concern for his wife and the idea of a world without her that some say overcame him. He couldn't imagine his life without her some said. But with her receiving first-rate care he focused as much attention as he could on the film. Though some said he lost a lot of the spark he had early on in the filming.

After 55-days, principal photography came to a close in October 1971 and Hitchcock was able to focus his attention on editing, post-production and other details. Hitchcock's cameo in the film would come, as usual, early on in the first major sequence when he appears in two crowd shots during the discovery of the first body in the river Thames along the Embankment.

Challenges for the Filmmaker

One of the key details that presented some challenge for the director was the film's score. For a more modern approach, Hitchcock hired composer Henry Mancini to provide the score for the film. Mancini had done this many times before, and earned Academy Awards for his scores on films *Days of Wine and Roses* and *Breakfast at Tiffany's*. But Hitchock's tradition was to use Bernard Herrmann, who had successfully scored many of the director's classics.

But after hearing portions of Mancini's completed score, Hitchcock reportedly said "If I had wanted Bernard Herrmann, I would have hired him!" Hitchcock then fired Mancini and hired British composer and conductor Ron Goodwin to complete the film's score.

Hitchcock also had his own challenges, once again, with the censors. While he was able to deliver much more than a decade earlier on *Psycho*, some of his graphic shots of the murder sequences include more nudity and required some attention. It was reportedly only the second film of Hitchcock's ever to receive cuts. The first being *Psycho*.

Film censor Stephen Murphy, who approved the release of Stanley Kubrick's *A Clockwork Orange* without cuts, felt that *Frenzy* needed "just a couple of little trims," according to the director.

"I am not given to goriness you know," Hitchcock told the press. "Frankly it was just a matter of degree in one death scene — a death by strangulation which I suppose you could describe as, well, somewhat protracted. The cuts are a matter of frames rather than seconds."

It was not surprising that Hitchcock took the treatment in stride. In fact, he would use the event as a chance to gain attention for the film and make moviegoers wonder what Hitchcock had in store for them. "These things are always a matter of degree, and it always depends on whether you do it with taste or not," said Hitchcock. "I made *Psycho* in black and white to avoid showing red blood. If I had made it in color it would have been horrible. When I made *Topaz* a London critic told me I was being modest. But I do not get seriously censored, because I have enough experience in this business to know what is sensible."

The Release

It was the first time the director would receive an MPAA "R" rating on a film when it was released in June 1972. It premiered in London on May 25, 1972 and Hitchcock was pleased to be able to attend the premiere alongside his wife Alma who had greatly improved after her stroke the previous year. And Hitchcock once again found he was a darling of the critics and moviegoers who largely responded very favorably to the film.

ALFRED HITCHCOCK: the icon years

At a budget of a mere $2 million, Universal was also thrilled with the film grossing some $6.5 million in the U.S. and Canada alone. It would go on to earn a reported $16 million in worldwide revenues. Hitchcock would use his own name and face, much like he did with *Psycho* to promote the film. While in *Psycho* he offered potential viewers a tour of the Bates Motel, in *Frenzy* they found him floating face up in the Thames as he offered them some insight into the gruesome goings-on in his new feature.

Film Quarterly summed up the film by writing "Alfred Hitchcock's latest film, is indeed triumphant in almost every way, and it is a cause for jubilation among those who admire suspense-thrillers. It is filmed in the London of today, but without the "trendy" atmosphere of the Beatles-Twiggy mob. It is, rather nostalgically, the enduring, everyday London of Covent Garden, Tottenham Court Road and the Embankment - sunny London, really, where commonplaces of traffic, banalities and dignities of language and behavior can camouflage the activities of a savage rapist-strangler who compulsively snuffs out the lives of women by day or night. Armed only with a necktie, the murderer terrorizes the city, with nonchalant, incurable dementia."

And *The Times of London* called Hitchcock "A great director again making a film worthy of his great talents; the magic remains intact." While *The Hollywood Reporter* said "Hitchcock seems to delight in making us aware of his craftsmanship – technique is flaunted the way it is in *Blowup*." *Newsday* found that "Hitchcock is in fine form in *Frenzy*," and Roger Ebert of the *Chicago Sun Times* agreed writing "A return to old form by the master of suspense." *Rolling Stone* went as far as to say it was a fully "retrospective" film as a culmination of his "entire body of work." *Time* magazine though perhaps put it best writing, "Hitchcock's *Frenzy* is the dazzling proof that anyone who makes a suspense film is still an apprentice to this old master."

In fact, Hitchcock's ability to create modern-day suspense thriller that had expansive location shooting instead of projection shots, paired with a modern and at times graphic story with characters squarely set in the 1970s showed Hitchcock as a current filmmaker. He had few contemporaries left in the business. His competition was a younger breed now and he was able to show the world he could keep up with anything the new style directors could come up with. And he could do it with the Hitchcock flair and style.

A Surprise Critic

However, not everyone was thrilled. Arthur La Bern, author of the novel on which the film was based was so disappointed with the resulting movie that he publicly slammed the director and screenwriter in the British Press.

In a letter to the *Times of London* in May 1972, shortly after the newspaper positively reviewed the film, La Bern wrote his own assessment of the feature in a letter to the editor.

"Sir, I wish I could share John Russell Taylor's enthusiasm for Hitchcock's distasteful film, *Frenzy*. I endured 116 minutes of it at a press showing and it was, at least to me, a most painful experience," wrote La Bern.

After explaining he was the author of the book the story was based on, he further went on to say, "The result on the screen is appalling. The dialogue is a curious amalgam of an old Aldwych farce, *Dixon of Dock Green* and that almost forgotten *No Hiding Place*. I would like to ask Mr. Hitchcock and Mr. Shaffer what happened between book and script to the authentic London characters I created."

He concluded by saying "I wish to dissociate myself with Mr. Shaffer's grotesque misrepresentation of Scotland Yard offices."

Hitchcock was also sued by a French playwright who claimed audiences would confuse the film with his play, *Frénésie*. Though the film held no similarities to his play the lawsuit claimed the director/producer had no right to use the name without the playwright's permission. In 1973, Hitchcock would settle the case by paying 150,000 francs, which came out to about £12,500. Hitchcock was also denied the use of the French word "Frénésie" in any publicity surrounding the release of the film in France.

But the film's success continued and *Frenzy* was selected as one of the four American films at the Cannes Film Festival in 1972. In fact, *Frenzy* was selected to close the festival that year. And while Hitchcock was denied an Academy Award nomination his film did pick up four Golden Globe nominations from the Foreign Press including one for Best Director. Hitchcock was also honored by the Hollywood Foreign Press Association with a special Golden Globe for his "outstanding contributions to the entertainment field."

ALFRED HITCHCOCK: the icon years

ALFRED HITCHCOCK: the icon years

sixteen

ALFRED HITCHCOCK: the icon years

ALFRED HITCHCOCK: the icon years

"Mystery is like a crossword puzzle, Suspense is emotional."
Alfred Hitchcock

Family Plot

Hitchcock digs up a new tale of suspense and intrigue

When asked about retirement in 1972, Hitchcock reportedly said, "I cannot retire. What would I do? I have no hobbies, so I will have to see where the next body turns up."

And thus with *Frenzy* receiving the acclaim he had sought for the past decade he would embark on a search for his next project. Hitchcock also had a contractual agreement with Universal that had him down for two more films for the studio and they had no intention of allowing him to break free of his contract. With the success of *Frenzy* the studio was once again proud to have Hitchcock in their stable and confident of him as a bankable star and commodity.

Another Honor

While Hitchcock celebrated in the success of his most recent film and contemplated what would be next, he was once again honored with a glowing retrospective of his work in January 1973 when the Los Angeles County Museum of Modern Art, in cooperation with the American Film Institute, offered "Presenting Alfred Hitchcock." The exhibition offered 21 of Hitchcock's classic features, starting with *Rear Window* and ending roughly a month later with his most recent work, *Frenzy*. It also included nine episodes he directed of his decade-long television series.

And in March that year he was again honored, this time by the International Alliance of Theatrical Stage Employees who presented him with an award for Motion Picture Showmanship during a luncheon in Hollywood.

By the spring Hitch was still reading books and looking for recommendations for an appropriate project when he was presented with a novel by English author Victor Canning called *The Rainbird Pattern*. The story was comfortable ground for the director as it had all the standard elements audiences might expect but did lack some of the gruesomeness of several of his biggest hits. The original title of the film was intended to be *One Plus One Equals One* when it was announced what Hitchcock's next picture would be, sometime in 1973. But perhaps because of confusion or the suspense-less sound of the name, Hitchcock decided to change the title when production was set in early 1975. By then the title had changed to something more familiar – a one-word catchier name – *Deceit*.

The film production would mark Hitchcock's 50th anniversary as a director and his 53rd feature film. Hitchcock once again turned to his old friend Ernest Lehman to help with the screenplay after Anthony Shaffer, whom he had worked with on the recent *Frenzy*, turned him down. Lehman, best known for his work on *North by Northwest*, hadn't worked with Hitch in some time and found that with the passing of years the director had slowed down quite a bit. While that was expected, he also noted the he was often much less interested in the development of the film than he had been in years prior.

A Film of Deception

In any event, a series of story conferences took place in November 1973 and a script, for a film now called *Deception*, would come forth in April 1974.

Lehman recalled that what drew Hitchcock to the story was how two distinct stories – one of a pair of kidnappers and jewel thieves would unfold alongside another story surrounding an heir to a fortune who was given up for adoption at birth and was now being sought by a pair of bungling would-be detectives – would come together in a dramatic and suspenseful manner. Universal provided the director with a budget of $3.5 million and Hitchcock had his usual complete control over the entire production, including final cut approval.

Hitchcock changed the story from the English countryside of the novel to modern day Los Angeles. It was a way to keep costs down as well as keep the story urban and current. Location shooting centered mostly in Southern California with filming in Pasadena and Los Angeles. Interiors were shot on the Universal soundstages and the furthest location shooting was only San Francisco, a few hours north of Hollywood.

For casting, once again Hitchcock steered away from costly stars and selected competent but less familiar actors. It would again allow him to retain star billing on his film, but enable the production to move smoothly with actors who knew their way around a large movie set. Barbara Harris was mostly familiar to audiences from her small screen appearances and guest spots on television shows. She came to Hitchcock's attention as far back as 1961 when she had a role in an episode of his *Alfred Hitchcock Presents* series.

Bruce Dern was also more familiar to viewers for his television appearances, though he had some notable supporting roles on the big screen in features like *Hush Hush Sweet Charlotte* in 1964 and *They Shoot Horses Don't They?* in 1969. He too worked on Hitchcock's TV show, with two roles in 1964 on *The Alfred Hitchcock Hour*. He would then have a small but key role in the climax of *Marnie* that same year. Dern claimed that Al Pacino was the studio's first choice for the role, but Hitchcock didn't want to pay his fee, and since he'd worked with him before Dern was offered the part.

Harris and Dern play a psychic and tax driver who are lovers in hopes of earning a finder's fee for locating a child given up for adoption who is now worthy of a large inheritance.

The other two central roles on the companion story line are another set of lovers who use kidnapping as a means of acquiring wealth and rare diamonds. Karen Black, who would be on a hot streak during the period for roles in *Five Easy Pieces, The Great Gatsby, Airport '75,* and *Day of the Locust* was probably the most familiar face in the production. Black recalled that she originally wanted the part of the psychic, but Hitchcock wouldn't agree to that and therefore she was offered and accepted the other female lead.

William Devane was the last of the four stars and was again mostly known for television appearances on shows like *Ironside, Mannix, Hawaii Five-O* and *Medical Center.* In fact, Devane was actually Hitchcock's first choice, but wasn't available when production was slated to begin, so another actor was chosen. Roy Thinnes was hired for the role but Hitchcock wasn't happy with his performance and replaced him with Devane shortly after filming began when he found out that Devane was available. So reshoots were required early on in production. Thinnes reportedly confronted Hitchcock in San Francisco one evening after being dismissed from the film as the director dined as a local restaurant. Hitch hated awkward situations, and just waited for Thinnes to finish and leave. He didn't enjoy making a scene in a crowded San Francisco restaurant. William Devane recalled that Thinnes actually appears in the film in some of the longer shots at Grace Cathedral in San Francisco.

A Milestone

On August 12, 1974 hundreds of members of the national and foreign press, along with Hollywood friends and celebrities once again paid tribute to Hitchcock. This time it was in honor of his 75th birthday. It was an event at Chasen's restaurant, hosted by chairman of MCA Universal Lew Wasserman.

Development of the film moved slowly through the spring and summer of 1974 and production was expected to begin in early 1975. Hitchcock was once again honored that spring for his achievements on film by the Film Society of Lincoln Center and traveled to New York for the festivities.

Hitchcock's wife Alma was once again in frail health and the director spent much of his summer caring for her and questioning her doctors to ensure she was getting the best of care. Alma had suffered both a bought with cancer as well as lingering issues from a stroke.

That fall he began to suffer some of his own health troubles. His weight had put him at the heaviest he'd ever been and he began to suffer dizziness and heart troubles.

Doctors inserted a pacemaker into him and medication he was prescribed affected him unexpectedly when he suffered a bout of colitis. No sooner had he begun to recover from that when they found he had a kidney stone. He also began to suffer more seriously from arthritis. Production was postponed until March 1975.

Hitch would use a second unit crew to direct most of the action related sequences like the car chase scene in the hills of Los Angeles.

Filming Begins

Filming finally began in spring 1975 and Bruce Dern recalled his work with Hitchcock by saying "I've never worked with anyone who proceeded so methodically. For Hitchcock, movement is dramatic. Not acting. When he wants the audience emotionally moved, the camera moves. He's a subtle man and he also the best actor I've ever worked with."

Filming was wrapping up at the end of July 1975 when the studio and the director were still trying to nail down a proper title for the film. Universal's publicity department reportedly suggested *Family Plot* and Hitchcock, unable to find anything better, agreed to the name.

At nearly 77-years old Hitchcock elected to do his cameo as a silouette behind a glass mainly because his health had caused him to look far worse than he had hoped and cortisone shots had left his face puffier than normal. Hitchcock's health would continue to deteriorate as post-production took over and his wife's health also took a turn for the worse when she suffered another stroke. Even so, Hitchcock and his production team were able to complete the film by early 1976.

The world premiere was held in March 1976 at the Filmex Festival in Los Angeles and opened into wider release that April. It again did well in its initial release, pulling in more than $13.2 million in the U.S.

The Times of London responded favorably to the film saying, "Alfred Hitchcock has yielded to age none of his mastery as storyteller. He still possesses the supreme gift of suspense, in the sense of sustaining, at every moment, curiosity about what comes next. Because it's played for light comedy going on farce, *Family Plot* risks being pigeon-holed as a frolic, a minor work in the old master's canon. Time, I guess, may well accord it a central place. It has the geometric ingenuity of the later American work, along with the delight in quirky character that marked Hitchcock's British period."

The *New Yorker* wrote "Hitchcock has never made a strategically wittier film, or a fonder; and this in his seventy-seventh year." And the *Los Angeles Times* called the film "... atmospheric, characterful, precisely paced, intricately plotted, exciting and suspenseful, beautifully acted."

While not all the reviews were glowing, the film fared quite well as a follow-up to *Frenzy* and moviegoers were satisfied with Hitchcock's latest delivery. Everyone now wondered if the director had anything else up his sleeve and Universal still had him contractually obligated for one more film.

ALFRED HITCHCOCK: the icon years

ALFRED HITCHCOCK: the icon years

seventeen

ALFRED HITCHCOCK: the icon years

ALFRED HITCHCOCK: the icon years

"If I made Cinderella, the audience would immediately be looking for a body in the coach."

Alfred Hitchcock

The Short Night

From 1976 until 1979 Hitchcock works on a final project

After *Family Plot*, Hitchcock was still a viable commodity and a filmmaker with clout in Hollywood. In fact, at a cost of roughly $3 million and a box office draw of more than $13 million in the United States alone, the success would enable Hitchcock to continue to develop projects as long as he was physically able.

As a filmmaker Hitchcock was always working on an idea. Even on the off years, when a film wasn't in some stage of development, as an avid reader Hitch would continually look at new or even old novels for ideas of potential films. And for many years he frequented the theater and kept and eye on the competition, in both the U.S. and Europe, to see what others were doing and look for inspiration from any source. Even the newspaper headlines proved useful for projects like *Psycho* and *The Birds*.

However, not all of Hitchcock's ideas or projects came to fruition as a finished product. Some of his film ideas, like *No Bail for the Judge, The Mary Deare,* and *Mary Rose* worked their way through the process, but were blocked from completion for one reason or another. Overall, there have been more than a dozen reported projects that Hitchcock spent time developing. As far back as 1939, when he tried to get the novel *Greenmantle* made into a film starring Cary Grant and Ingrid Bergman, or even sooner if you consider that *Mary Rose* was a play he saw in the 1920s and would try for years to turn the idea into film.

The Short Night

Hitchcock's last unfinished film to conclude his Universal contract was intended to be based on a spy novel by Ronald Kirkbride entitled *The Short Night*. It was an espionage thriller that Hitchcock had crafted into a screenplay with the idea of it being his follow-up feature to *Family Plot*.

Based loosely on the true story of a British double agent named George Blake, the tale follows his escape from prison as he flees to Finland with plans to eventually reach Moscow. He expects to meet up with his wife and children who are waiting for him. In the meantime, an American agent, whose brother was one of the double agent's victims, is on his trail arrives in Finland, hoping to intercept him. However, the agent ends up falling in love with the wife of the traitor that leads to complications and a series of unexpected twists and turns.

Cut from the cloth of *Torn Curtain* and *Topaz*, the film represented a chance for Hitchcock to "get it right" at last and produce a first-rate espionage suspense thriller. Potential leading men who were being considered for the main male roles included Clint Eastwood, Walter Matthau, and Sean Connery, while Liv Ullman was reportedly approached about playing the double agent's wife.

The first writer assigned to the picture didn't see eye to eye with the director/producer and bowed out early on, so Hitchcock once again turned to Ernest Lehman, the writer who had helped bail Hitchcock out numerous times before on difficult projects. But Lehman felt the story's focus should come from the perspective of the American agent and Hitchcock disagreed. So Hitchcock turned to another old friend, Norman Lloyd, who he had worked with on *Saboteur* many years before, after Leaman left the project. But Hitchcock wanted to quickly draft screenplay before all the elements of the story were worked out. When Lloyd objected Hitchcock decided to do the screenplay himself and reportedly fired Lloyd in a fit of anger.

The Director's Health

Universal was a bit concerned that Hitchcock's failing health and advanced years would prevent the film from ever being made and was unsure he was up to the task. Hitchcock eventually agreed that he needed the help of a qualified writer and accepted Universal's offer of using David Freeman. Freeman helped Hitchcock iron out the story and produce a screenplay. A final draft was submitted and approved by the director in the fall of 1978 and it was this draft Hitchcock had Freeman modify.

However, the story goes that is was during pre-production for the film in 1979 that Hitchcock realized that his declining health would make directing the film impossible so he asked old friend Hilton Green break the news to Universal that he had decided to retire. Hitchcock would close the book on *The Short Night* and would never complete another film.

Hitchcock would reluctantly retire as he realized his health was deteriorating and he no longer had the stamina to endure a lengthy development and production schedule. He also didn't have the strength to scout or film on the lengthy location shoots his films often required, nor could be deal with actors and crew as effectively as he had in the past. His contract with Universal still left him with one film to deliver, but Hitchcock realized he would never fulfill his contractual agreement with Universal. And the studio knew there was little they could do as the director was nearing the end of his life.

ALFRED HITCHCOCK: the icon years

eighteen

ALFRED HITCHCOCK: the icon years

ALFRED HITCHCOCK: the icon years

"They say that when a man drowns his entire life flashes before his eyes. I am indeed fortunate for having just had that same experience without even getting my feet wet."

Alfred Hitchcock

One Last Honor

The American Film Institute offers Hitchcock its Lifetime Achievement Award

While Hitchcock still had a lingering hope that he still had one film left in him – the one that would complete his contractual agreement with Universal – he was once again given an honor for his dedication to the world of cinema. The American

Film Institute had selected him as the seventh recipient of their Lifetime Achievement Award.

Looking Back at a Career

It was announced in the fall of 1978 that he would receive the honor, but the iconic director provided little help in preparing the event. Nor did he offer to help arrange or participate in press interviews. He wouldn't even help select the clips from his movies that would be used in the event.

Some suspected he didn't want to take part in an event that signaled an end to his career. Others in his camp tried to suggest he was still busy with his own plans for an upcoming film, too busy to spend his time looking back at the past. But still, others knew his failing health also prevented him from getting too involved in any major venture at this point. "He looked on the evening as his own obituary," David Freeman told author Donald Spoto. "And he didn't want to attend the funeral."

In any event, on March 7, 1979, at the Beverly Hilton Hotel, 150 dining tables held a collection of Hollywood stars from past and present. They paid $300 for a four-course dinner and a chance to honor the legendary icon Alfred Hitchcock. It was a major Hollywood event, complete with an Academy Awards-like entrance, lights, cameras and action and the evening would be captured for airing on national television.

Many who had worked with the director, including James Stewart, Ingrid Bergman, Cary Grant, Janet Leigh, Jane Wyman, Joan Fontaine, Dame Judith Anderson, Tippi Hedren, Sean Connery, Vera Miles, Theresa Wright, Rod Taylor and others joined a host of other celebrities like Charlton Heston, Diana Ross, Michael Caine, Christopher Reeve, Barbra Streisand, Mel Brooks and many more to pay tribute, roast, and thank the man who gave so much to genre of film.

Hitchcock arrived for the ceremony much earlier in the day and relaxed in a suite on the 7th floor waiting for the festivities to begin. It was earlier in the day that he also taped his acceptance remarks. So later, if his health made it difficult for him to muster up the strength, he would still appear vital.

Later in the day, his wife Alma would arrive. She was initially not expected to attend, according to news reports. Her health was as frail, if not worse, than that of her husband. A series of strokes had left her with limited mobility, but she was determined to attend.

A Recorded TV Event

When the lights went up the images that appeared on screen were that of the director, many years earlier, from one of his infamous television experiences. It was the dry dark humor the world had come to expect.

Ingrid Bergman acted as the Mistress of Ceremonies and the evening that followed centered on clips from many of his most memorable movies, along with table-side monologues from those that starred in them talking about what it was like to work for the master. Bergman told Hitch, "We want to thank you for all the fun and the feat you have given us." She also fondly recalled arguing with him once about not being able to give him the emotion he was looking for in a scene and she recalled him giving her some advice. "Ingrid, fake it," he told her. She said it was the best advice she had received and she would use it often over her long career.

Bergman also made reference to the possibility that there might be another Hitchcock film. In introducing Ernest Lehman, Bergman said he was at work with Hitch on his next picture. Whether the reference was purely fiction to give the impression that Hitchcock was still at work or whether he still actually believed he would complete another film, it was clear from the evening that Hitchcock was becoming less mobile and his ability to direct a feature film was in question.

Hitchcock was very reserved throughout the evening. He reportedly offered the bulk of his comments during the event privately to his wife and appeared uninterested and unwilling to accept guests and visitors at his table. The only ones who would be able to truly say they dined with him that evening were the few that sat at his table – his wife Alma, alongside Gary Grant, James Stewart, his agent Lew Wasserman, one of his oldest friends Sidney Bernstein, and Ingrid Bergman.

The event was broadcast on television five evenings later and the world had a chance to pay its own tribute to the master of suspense.

ALFRED HITCHCOCK: the icon years

nineteen

ALFRED HITCHCOCK: the icon years

ALFRED HITCHCOCK: the icon years

"They tell me a murder is committed every minute, so I don't want to waste any more of your time. In know you want to get to work."

Alfred Hitchcock

The End

The passing of a legend and icon

Hitchcock had been in failing health during the last year of his life. At 80, he was still severely overweight and his size combined with arthritis and general complications that come as a man of his age, made living difficult. He was aware the end was near and spoke of it to those close to him.

In January of 1980 he was named a Knight Commander of the

British Empire by Queen Elizabeth. The announcement of the honor was actually made over Christmas 1979, at about the same time he was named Man of the Year by the British-American Chamber of Commerce.

With his health frail, the ceremony took place at Universal Studios. And even though Hitchcock had officially retired from Universal and his offices there had been dismantled, the event was held on a "set" created to give the appearance that Hitchcock was just having a "usual day at the office."

Hitchcock even rose to the occasion and spoke to the press of the knighthood. "I suppose it shows that if you stick at something long enough eventually somebody takes note." And when asked if he thought it would make his wife treat him differently now that he was Sir Alfred Hitchcock, he joked, "I certainly hope so. Perhaps she will now mind her own business and do what she's told."

A luncheon to celebrate the knighthood was held that afternoon and Cary Grant and Janet Leigh were among those who attended and once again honored the icon.

His Last Appearance

His last public appearance was in March 1980 when he was escorted to the Beverly Hilton Hotel to announce the recipient of the next American Film Institute Lifetime Achievement Award. It was customary for the previous year's recipient to announce the next one. In this instance it was especially poignant – the recipient was James Stewart. So Hitchcock gathered up his strength and taped his opening remarks to be delivered at the ceremony. Though his ill health prevented him from attending the actual event.

As April progressed doctor visits to his home grew more and more frequent as his health declined and his wife's health also suffered. On the evening of April 28, his family and those closest to him gathered. Doctors knew that the end was near. On April 29, 1980, at 9:17 a.m., Alfred Hitchcock died of kidney failure in his Los Angeles home at the age of 80.

His wife Alma would die two years later at the age of 82. They would leave a daughter, Patricia Hitchcock O'Connell, an actress who had been on the screen in several of Hitchcock's pictures, appearing in both *Strangers on a Train* and *Psycho*, as well as a small walk-on part and double for Jane Wyman in *Stage Fright*. She would carry on Hitchcock's name and help oversee his estate and maintain his legacy.

His last project, as previously mentioned, was the script for his intended spy thriller, based on *The Short Night*. The script was eventually published posthumously, in a book on Hitchcock's last years.

The funeral service was held at Good Shepherd Catholic Church in Beverly Hills and Hitchcock's body was cremated and his ashes were scattered over the Pacific.

His estate was estimated in excess of $20 million and included numerous real estate holdings, government bonds, oil and gas wells, more than 2,000 head of cattle and 150,0000 shares of MCA stock. His wife and daughter would receive the bulk of his estate, but a complicated series of trusts had been set up to manage the intricacies of the income from his films and other works and to help ensure the legacy he had created.

ALFRED HITCHCOCK: the icon years

ALFRED HITCHCOCK: the icon years

twenty

ALFRED HITCHCOCK: the icon years

ALFRED HITCHCOCK: the icon years

"Always make the audience suffer as much as possible."
Alfred Hitchcock

Closing Remarks

An icon for the generations to discover and rediscover

Francois Truffaut once remarked, "Hitchcock revels in being misunderstood, more so because it is on misunderstandings that he has constructed his life."

The statement perhaps helps explain why the public has endured such a long and at time complex love affair with the man. One biographer suggested that "he's a man who always looks like he just come from a funeral," describing him with his "rotund Santa Claus like body," always dressed in a "navy blue suit, white shirt, and banker's tie."

But beyond the unassuming and never-threatening appearance

was a complicated man whose humor was dark, biting, cold, droll, dry and fraught with innuendo. He was fascinated by sex and murder. His work stands testament to the gruesomeness of life and the macabre behavior of the everyday man. It was if he was saying "yes, I'm fascinated by this, but you're doing it," or "you're an accomplice for being as fascinated by it as I am."

His career covered the bizarre and focused our attention on it and people began to expect it and look forward to it. He once said "If I made Cinderella, the audience would start looking for the body in the pumpkin coach." He went on to assume "If an audience sees one of my productions with no spine-tingling, they're disappointed. " And he was right, we were.

Films for the Ages

As an icon his image and what he stood for lives on. His films still earn acclaim and attention – and money. In 1998 when the American Film Institute (AFI) released its list of the 100 greatest movies of all time, Hitchcock hit the list four times. The films were judged on a variety of criteria including their cultural impact, historical significance, popularity and awards and critical recognition, among others. Three of his films came in the top 50. *Vertigo* came in at 61 on the list while *Rear Window* landed at 42, *North by Northwest* at 40 and his 1960 classic *Psycho* came in at 18. He should have made the top ten, but Hitchcock was denied an Academy Award as best director, even with five nominations. So the criteria of the judging affected his place in the AFI history books.

He was first nominated for an Academy Award for *Rebecca*, and although the film would go on to earn best picture, surprisingly enough, he was not awarded a statuette, when John Ford took the award for *Grapes of Wrath* instead. He was nominated again for *Lifeboat* in 1944, but would lose to Leo McCary and that year's best picture *Going My Way*.

Two years later, in 1946, he would again be nominated, this time for *Spellbound*. But he lost again when Billy Wilder took home best director and best picture for *The Lost Weekend*.

In 1955, when *On The Waterfront* took 1954's best picture, it also came away with a best director award for its director Elia Kazan and Hitchcock again lost when he was nominated for *Rear Window*. And at last, in 1961, when many thought it would be the director's moment to shine, he once again found his work nominated when *Psycho* earned him a spot for best director. But he would lose this time to Billy Wilder who's best picture and best director wins for *The Apartment* would deny Hitchcock his last chance at winning an Oscar.

A Lasting Impression

In 1967 The Academy of Motion Pictures Arts and Sciences would attempt to right its wrong by honoring Hitchcock with its Irving Thalberg Award. The Irving Thalberg Award is presented to a filmmaker who's impressive credentials are long overdue for formal recognition from his or her peers. Such was certainly the case when Hitchcock received the award.

Since then his work has continued to astound moviegoers and his life and career have been evaluated and re-evaluated. Some writers have glossed over Hitchcock's later years, suggesting his work after *Psycho* was merely a downward spiral, but those assessments miss the mark. As a seasoned filmmaker Hitchcock was evaluated on a standard above many others. His later films offer glimpses of greatness and continue to reward with repeated viewings. And those films are still being re-evaluated within the scope of his entire career.

And while Hitchcock was certainly not without his flaws, his cinematic achievements are beyond impressive. His treatment of his actors, including a number of his leading ladies was less than perfect, and at times downright harassment. But what he and his collaborators left on celluloid offer us cinematic gems.

In fact, considering Hitchcock's Hollywood films, from *Rebecca* through *Family Plot*, it's estimated that Hitchcock's work grossed more than $223 million. It's an impressive amount when one considers tickets prices at movie houses for many of the years he was releasing films was less than 50 cents and even by 1976 when his final film was released the average ticket was less than $2.50.

And still they keep on earning. DVD releases and theatrical re-releases of his films still garner attention. And he is still one of the most recognizable names and faces in Hollywood's long and illustrious history. History will continue to be kind to Alfred Hitchcock, the filmmaker. For we love our icons and Hitchcock, the director, is truly one of the best.

ALFRED HITCHCOCK: the icon years

Appendix

ALFRED HITCHCOCK: the icon years

ALFRED HITCHCOCK: the icon years

"Give them pleasure - the same pleasure they have when they wake up from a nightmare."

Alfred Hitchcock

Filmography

The Films of Alfred Hitchcock in reverse chronological order.

1970s

- ❋ Family Plot (1976)

- ❋ Frenzy (1972)

ALFRED HITCHCOCK: the icon years

1960s

- Topaz (1969)
- Torn Curtain (1966)
- Marnie (1964)
- The Birds (1963)
- "The Alfred Hitchcock Hour" (1 episode, 1962)
- "Alfred Hitchcock Presents" (17 episodes, 1955-1961)
- Psycho (1960)
- "Ford Star Time" (1 episode, 1960)

1950s

- North by Northwest (1959)
- Vertigo (1958)
- "Suspicion" (1 episode, 1957)
- The Wrong Man (1956)
- The Man Who Knew Too Much (1956)
- The Trouble with Harry (1955)

ALFRED HITCHCOCK: the icon years

* To Catch a Thief (1955)

* Rear Window (1954)

* Dial M For Murder (1954)

* I Confess (1953)

* Strangers on a Train (1951)

* Stage Fright (1950)

1940s

* Under Capricorn (1949)

* Rope (1948)

* The Paradine Case (1947)

* Notorious (1946)

* Spellbound (1945)

* Watchtower Over Tomorrow (1945) (uncredited)

* The Fighting Generation (1944) (uncredited)

* Lifeboat (1944)

ALFRED HITCHCOCK: the icon years

- Aventure malgache (1944)
- Bon Voyage (1944)
- Shadow of a Doubt (1943)
- Saboteur (1942)
- Suspicion (1941)
- Mr. & Mrs. Smith (1941)
- Foreign Correspondent (1940)
- Rebecca (1940)

1930s

- Jamaica Inn (1939)
- The Lady Vanishes (1938)
- Young and Innocent (1937)
- Sabotage (1936)
- Secret Agent (1936)
- The 39 Steps (1935)
- The Man Who Knew Too Much (1934)

ALFRED HITCHCOCK: the icon years

* Waltzes from Vienna (1934)

* Number Seventeen (1932)

* Rich and Strange (1931)

* Mary (1931)

* The Skin Game (1931)

* Murder! (1930)

* Juno and the Paycock (1930)

* An Elastic Affair (1930)

* Elstree Calling (1930) (provided sketches)

1920s

* The Manxman (1929)

* Blackmail (1929)

* Champagne (1928)

* Easy Virtue (1928)

* The Farmer's Wife (1928)

ALFRED HITCHCOCK: the icon years

- Downhill (1927)

- The Ring (1927)

- The Lodger: A Story of the London Fog (1927)

- The Mountain Eagle (1926)

- The Pleasure Garden (1925)

- Always Tell Your Wife (1923) (uncredited)

- Number 13 (1922) (unfinished)

"I have great respect for crime and the people involved with it, and such being the case, I deplore the careless crime. It has no finesse, no sense of balance, no feeling of accomplishment."

Alfred Hitchcock

Sources

Selected Bibliograpy

A number of books, magazines, newspapers, documentaries and interviews, as well as the films themselves provided sources of information and factual data that went into the writing of this book. Thank you to the many sources referenced throughout the book. There were many individuals whose work, insights, reviews, comments and suggestions that also helped make this book possible.

Books

Campbell, Robert. *The Golden Years of Broadcasting*. 1976. New York. Rutledge Books.

Finler, Joel W. *The Hollywood Story*. 1988. New York. Crown Publishers, Inc.

Harris, Robert A., Lasky, Michael S. *The Films of Alfred Hitchcock*. 1976. New York. Citadel Press.

Hingham, Charles. *Audrey - The Life of Audrey Hepburn*. 1984. Macmillan Publishing Company.

Hirschhorn, Clive. *The Universal Story*. 1983. New York. Crown Publishers, Inc.

Humphries, Patrick. *The Films of Alfred Hitchcock*. 1986. New Jersey. Crescent Books.

Hunter, Evan. *Me and Hitch*. 1997. London and Boston. Faber and Faber

Jones, Stephen. *Clive Barker's A-Z of Horror*. 1997. New York. HarperPrism.

Kapsis, Robert E. *Hitchcock: The Making of a Reputation*. 1992. Chicago. The University of Chicago Press.

Kraft, Jeff and Leventhal, Aaron. *Footsteps in the Fog*. 2002. Santa Monica Press.

Leigh, Janet. *Psycho – Behind the Scenes of the Classic Thriller.* 1996. New York. Harmony Books.

McCarty, John. *The Fearmakers.* 1994. New York. St. Martin's Press.

McCarty, John. *The Modern Horror Film.* 1990. New York. Citadel Press.

McCarty, John. *Psychos – Eighty Years of Mad Movies, Maniacs, and Murderous Deeds.* 1986. New York. St Martin's Press.

Moog, Ken. *The Alfred Hitchcock Story.* 1999. London. Titan Books.

Nelson, Nancy. *Evenings with Cary Grant.* 1991. New York. Warner Books.

Quirk, Lawrence. *The Films of Paul Newman.* 1971. New Jersey. Citadel Press.

Schoell, Willam. *Stay Out of the Shower* – 25 Years of Shocker Films Beginning with 'Psycho.' 1985. New York. Dembner Books.

Shulman, Arthur & Youman, Roger. *How Sweet It Was.* 1966. New York. Bonanza Books.

Spoto, Donald. *The Dark Side of Genius: The Life of Alfred Hitchcock.* 1983. New York. Ballantine Books.

Spoto, Donald. *The Art of Alfred Hitchcock.* 1992. New York. Anchor Books.

Sternfield, Jonathan. *The Look of Horror – Scary Moments from Scary Movies*. 1990. Philadelphia. M&M Books.

Sterritt, David. *The Films of Alfred Hitchcock*. 1993. New York. Cambridge University Press.

Stirling, Richard. *Julie Andrews – An Intimate Biography*. 2007. New York. St. Martin's Press.

Magazines, Newspapers

Coburn, Robert. "Fine Feathered Friends on a Rampage." Life Magazine. February 1, 1963.

Craft, Dan. "Diabolique." The Patangraph. August 15, 1997.

Curtis, Quentin. "Hitchcock the Romantic: His Films Famously Celebrated and Tortured Women." The Daily Telegraph." April 27, 1996.

Huard, Christine. "Actress Honored for Efforts to Protect Animals." The San Diego Union-Times. June 29, 1995.

Joiner, Lynne. "Star of 'The Birds' Preserves Lives of Wild Animals." CNN News. December 26, 1994

Kerh, Dave. "Marnie." The Chicago Tribune. October 23, 1986.

La Bern, Arthur. "Letters to the Editor: Hitchcock's 'Frenzy.'" The

Times of London. May 29, 1972.

Lee, Shirley. "Tippi Hedren: Nature Girl." Mature Health. October 1989.

Miller, Ron. "A Cool Blond Looks Back." The Chicago Tribune. March 24, 1994.

Morton, Tony. "She's at Home at the Zoo." Omaha World Herald. May 21, 1995.

Thomas, Bob. "Star of Hitchcock Thriller Keeps Blood Stirring In Own Private Jungle." Los Angeles Times. July 3, 1994.

Thomas, Bob. "Hollywood." Associated Press. August 6, 1979.

Internet Sources

The Alfred Hitchcock Wiki: www.hitchcockwiki.com

Wikipedia: www.wikipedia.com

The Internet Movie Database: www.imdb.com

The Numbers – Box Office Data, Movie Stars, Idle Speculation: www.the-numbers.com

Box Office Mojo: www.boxofficemojo.com

Photographic Credits

In addition to the selected bibliograpy of sources we would also like to acknowledge the many photographs used in this book. While many are part of the author's private collection, we would like to specifically acknowledge the following for illustrations used that are used for the purpose of review to highlight and complement the text:

Alfred Hitchcock Productions; Shamley Productions, Inc.; 20th Century Fox; United Artists, Universal; Sipa Press; Life Magazine; Cinema Photos; CinemaShop.

ALFRED HITCHCOCK: the icon years

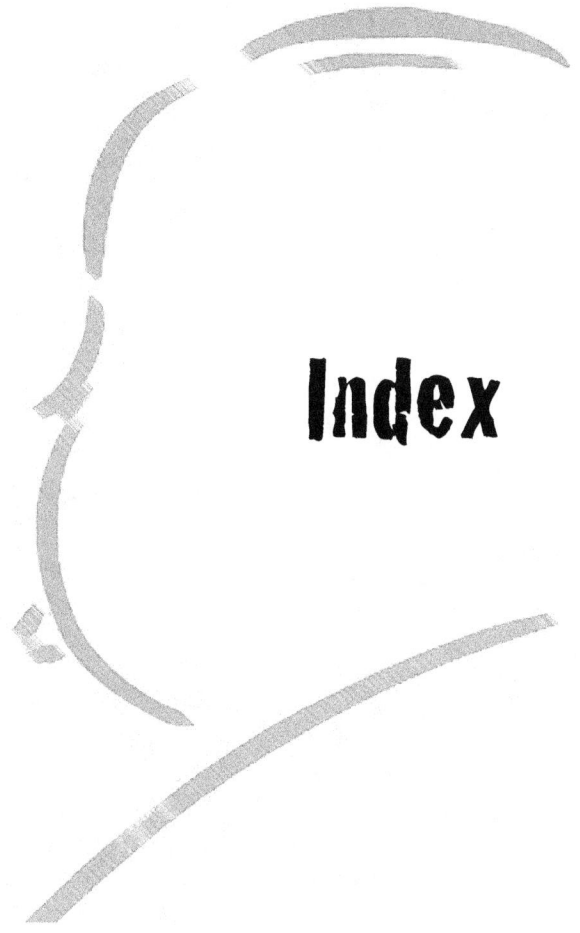

Index

ALFRED HITCHCOCK: the icon years

Index

A

Academy Award 26
Academy of Motion Pictures Arts and
    Sciences 129, 207
Academy of Motion Picture Arts and Sci-
    ences 146
Airport 75 180
Alfred Hitchcock Presents 24, 91
Allen, Irwin 1, 17, 231, 232
Allen, Jay Presson 97
Ambler, Eric 54
American Film Institute 160, 178, 193,
    200, 206
Anderson, Judith 194
Anderson, Michael 54
Andrews, Julie 129, 130, 131, 132, 133,
    134, 136, 138, 139, 144, 153, 220
A Clockwork Orange 170
A Countess From Hong Kong 90

A Nun's Story 44

B

BAFTA 44
Balsam, Martin 57
Bancroft, Anne 70
Bass, Saul 58
Bates, Michael 167
Battle Cry 152
Beatles, The 171
Beaty, David 66
Bergman, Ingrid 144, 154, 188, 194,
    195, 196
Bernstein, Sidney 196
Beverly Hilton Hotel 200
Black, Karen 180
Bloch, Robert 56
Bogart, Humphrey 44
Bogdanavich, Peter 78

Boston University 145
Breakfast at Tiffany's 169
British-American Chamber of Commerce 200
Brooks, Mel 194
Buchan, John 73
Bumstead, Henry 45
Butterfield 8 46
Bye Bye Birdie 60

C

Caine, Michael 161, 194
Cambridge University Film Society 145
Cannes Film Festival 71, 117, 173
Canning, Victor 178
Carpenter, John 61
Castle, William 56
CBS 32, 91
Cecil, Henry 46
Center for Advanced Film Studies 160
Chasen's restaurant 181
Chicago Sun Times 171
Chicago Tribune 91
Cinderella 187
Cinemascope 73
Clouzot, Henri-Georges 78
Coleman, Herbert 45, 153
Connery, Sean 89, 130, 153, 189, 194
Cool Hand Luke 131
Cooper, Gary 54
Cuban Missile Crisis 152
Curse of the Silver Screen 17
Curtis, Jamie Lee 61

D

Day, Doris 67, 85, 130
Days of Wine and Roses 169
Day of the Locust 180
Deceit (see Family Plot) 178
Deception (see Family Plot) 179
Dell Publishing 40

Deneuve, Catherine 153
Dern, Bruce 180, 182
Devane, William 180
Dial M For Murder 46
Directors Guild of Canada 146
Disney, Walt 62
Disneyland 62
Dixon of Dock Green 172
Dor, Karen 153
Dream On 90
du Maurier, Daphne 67

E

Eastwood, Clint 189
Edith Head 68
Ed Sullivan Show, The 32
Exodus 152

F

Family Plot 60, 126, 177, 182, 187, 188, 207, 211
Filmex Festival 182
Finch, Jon 167, 168
Five Easy Pieces 180
Fontaine, Joan 194
Ford, John 32, 206
Ford Star Time 32
Forsythe, John 153
Foster, Barry 167, 168
Foster, Georgia 55
Frankenheimer, John 78
Freeman, David 189, 194
Frenzy 60, 160, 161, 165, 166, 167, 170, 171, 172, 173, 177, 178, 179, 183, 211, 220
Friendly Persuasion 57

G

Gavin, John 57, 70, 118
Gein, Edward 55, 61
Going My Way 206
Golden Globe 60, 173

Goodwin, Ron 170
Good Shepherd Catholic Church 201
Grace Cathedral 181
Graham, Winston 86
Grant, Cary 39, 46, 49, 118, 130, 131, 138, 154, 167, 188, 194, 200, 219
Grapes of Wrath 206
Green, Hilton 189
Greenmantle 188
Griffith, Melanie 68, 90
Griffith, Richard 78
Griswold, Claire 98
Guy Burgess 132

H

Halloween H20: 20 years Later 61
Harper 131
Harvey, Laurence 46
Hawaii Five-O 180
Hawkes, Howard 78
Hedren, Tippi 17, 67, 73, 85, 89, 91, 98, 111, 112, 117, 118, 139, 194, 221
Hemmings, David 161
Hepburn, Audrey 44
Herrmann, Bernard 169
Heston, Charlton 54, 194
Hitchcock, Alfred 4, 7, 9, 15, 16, 17, 18, 23, 24, 26, 29, 31, 32, 37, 38, 39, 43, 46, 53, 54, 56, 65, 68, 77, 79, 83, 85, 91, 95, 98, 99, 117, 129, 130, 132, 133, 143, 145, 147, 151, 159, 165, 167, 171, 177, 178, 180, 182, 187, 193, 194, 199, 200, 205, 208, 211, 212, 217, 218, 219, 221, 222
Hitchcock, Alma 30, 67, 151, 169, 170, 181, 195, 196, 201
Hitchcock, Emma 29
Hitchcock, Patricia 30, 201
Hitchcock, William 29
Hitchcock: The Making of a Reputation 16
Holden, William 44
Hollywood Foreign Press Association 173
Hollywood Reporter, The 171
Houdini 57
How to Steal a Million 49
Hunter, Evan 69
Hush Hush Sweet Charlotte 180

I

Incrocci, Agenore 140
International Alliance of Theatrical Stage Employees 178
In the Deep Woods 61
Ironside 180
It Always Rains on Sunday 166
I Confess 26

J

James Bond 138, 153

K

Kael, Pauline 155
Kaleidoscope 161
Kapsis, Robert 16
Kazan, Elia 207
Kelly, Grace 67
Kirkbride, Ronald 188
Kramer, Stanley 57
Kubrick, Stanley 78

L

Landau, Martin 39
Landis, Jessie Royce 39
La Bern, Arthur 166, 172, 220
Lehman, Ernest 48, 54, 62, 179, 189, 195
Leigh, Janet 17, 24, 57, 58, 59, 60, 61,

66, 67, 85, 91, 105, 106, 144, 168, 194, 200, 218
Levy, Ben 161
Lifeboat 26, 31, 206, 213
Life magazine 138
Little Women 57
Lloyd, Norman 91, 189
London Film Society 146
Los Angeles Times 183, 221
Lucy 32

M

MacLean, Donald 132
Mancini, Henry 169
Mannix 180
Marnie 11, 66, 83, 85, 86, 87, 88, 89, 90, 91, 97, 98, 99, 117, 131, 138, 155, 180, 212, 220
Mary Rose 66, 87, 88, 89, 95, 96, 97, 98, 99, 100, 151, 188
Mason, James 39
Massey, Anna 167
Master of Disaster 17
Master of Suspense 17, 18, 84, 155
Matthau, Walter 189
MCA 56, 68, 92, 181, 201
McCary, Leo 206
McCowen, Alec 167
Medical Center 180
Merchant, Vivien 167
MGM 86
Miles, Vera 49, 57, 59, 67, 85, 108, 194
MOMA 79
Montand, Yves 153
Moore, Brian 133
Motion Picture Herald 130
Murphy, Stephen 170
Museum of Modern Art 71

N

NBC 32, 91
Newman, Paul 130, 131, 133, 136, 137, 139, 144, 152, 153, 219
New Yorker 183
New York Post 138
New York Repertory Theater 78
New York Times 26, 59, 79, 138, 154
Night of the Lepus 60
North by Northwest 24, 25, 31, 37, 39, 40, 45, 49, 53, 54, 67, 84, 179, 206, 212
Notorious 26
Novak, Kim 67
No Bail for the Judge 43, 44, 46, 49, 53, 56, 89, 188
No Hiding Place 172

O

One Plus One Equals One 178
On The Beach 57
On The Waterfront 207
Oscar 31, 44, 57, 60, 129, 130, 207

P

Pacific Heights 90
Pacino, Al 180
Paramount 47
Peck, Gregory 44
Perkins, Anthony 57, 58, 60, 61, 67
Perry Mason 98
Photoplay 88
Pleashette, Suzanne 70
Polanski, Roman 78
Princess Grace 67
Psycho 17, 18, 24, 25, 26, 53, 54, 56, 57, 58, 60, 61, 62, 65, 66, 67, 69, 70, 72, 83, 84, 85, 86, 89, 91, 92, 99, 105, 108, 112, 113, 161, 167, 168, 170, 171, 188, 201, 206, 207, 212, 218, 219
Psycho: Behind the Scenes of the Classic Thriller 17
Psycho II 24

Q

Queen Elizabeth 200

R

R.R.R.R. 139
Rear Window 26, 31, 38, 67, 84, 138, 178, 206
Rebecca 26, 31, 206, 207, 214
Redford, Robert 161
Reel Horror 17
Reeve, Christopher 194
Reville, Alma 30
Robbin, Dany 153
Rolling Stone 171
Roman Holiday 44
Room at the Top 46
Ross, Diana 194
Rossellini, Roberto 78

S

Saboteur 31, 189, 214
Sabrina 44, 46, 154
Saint, Eva Marie 39, 67, 85, 130
Saturday's Review 72
Scaramouche 57
Scarpelli, Furio 140
Scotland Yard 167, 172
Selznick, David O. 30, 31
Shadow of a Doubt 31, 161, 214
Shaffer, Anthony 167, 179
Shambala Preserve 90
Shamley Productions 32
Sinatra, Frank 46
Sleuth 167
Spellbound 16, 206, 213
Spellbound by Beauty: Alfred Hitchcock and His Leading Ladies 16
Spoto, Donald 15, 16, 137, 194, 219
Stafford, Frederick 153
Stage Fright 31, 39, 165, 201, 213

Stanley Kubrick 78, 170
Stewart, James 62, 194, 196, 200
Strangers on a Train 26
Streisand, Barbra 194
Suspicion 31, 32, 212, 214

T

Taylor, Gil 167
Taylor, John Russell 172
Taylor, Rod 70, 118, 139, 194
Taylor, Samuel 45, 48, 154, 161, 168
Technicolor 47
Thalberg, Irving 146, 207
They Shoot Horses Don't They? 180
The Alfred Hitchcock Hour 32, 91, 180, 212
The Apartment 207
The Birds 17, 60, 65, 66, 67, 68, 69, 70, 71, 72, 73, 77, 79, 84, 85, 86, 89, 90, 98, 111, 112, 113, 114, 117, 118, 139, 188, 212, 220
The Birds - Lands End 90
The Blind Man 62
The Bold and the Beautiful 90
The Dark Side of Genius 15
The Dick Powell Show 98
The DuPont Show of the Month 98
The Fog 61
The Great Gatsby 180
The Humane Society 70
The London Times 165
The Lost Weekend 207
The Manchurian Candidate 46
The Mary Deare 188
The Naked Spur 57
The Paradine Case 31
The Rainbird Pattern 178
The Screen Producers Guild 99
The Short Night 187, 188, 189, 201
The Sound of Music 129, 130
The Three Hostages 74
The Times of London 98, 171, 182,

The Trouble with Harry 39, 153, 212
The Twilight Zone 98
The Wreck of the Mary Deare 53
The Wrong Man 31
Thinnes, Roy 180, 181
Thomas, M. Robert 73
Through the Eyes of a Killer 90
Time magazine 59, 89
Topaz 151, 152, 153, 154, 155, 159, 166, 170, 188, 212
Torn Curtain 129, 130, 131, 133, 137, 138, 139, 143, 145, 152, 153, 155, 188, 212
To Catch a Thief 26, 46, 67, 84, 213
Trap for a Solitary Man 73
Truffaut, Francois 89, 99, 146, 147, 160, 205
Twentieth Century Fox 73
Twiggy 171

U

Under Capricorn 31
Universal 56, 71, 86, 89, 92, 99, 108, 112, 123, 130, 132, 133, 136, 137, 140, 147, 151, 152, 153, 154, 155, 161, 167, 171, 177, 179, 181, 182, 183, 188, 189, 190, 193, 200, 218
University of California 159
University of Southern California 160
Uris, Leon 152, 153, 154

V

Variety 72, 137
Vertigo 26, 31, 38, 47, 67, 78, 85, 91, 108, 139, 154, 206, 212
Village of Stars 66
VistaVision 47
Volpe, John 145

W

Waltzes of Vienna 96

Wasserman, Lew 72, 99, 181, 196
Wayne, John 130
Welles, Orson 78
Whitlock, Albert 97
Wilder, Billy 78, 206, 207
Williams, John 46
Worden, Bernice 55
Wright, Theresa 194
Wyman, Jane 194, 201

About the Author

John William Law is a writer and journalist whose work has appeared in newspapers, magazines and books. He has worked on the staffs of daily, weekly and monthly publications. He is the author of numerous books and narrates a podcast on iTunes entitled *The Movie Files*. He has appeared on television and film documentaries discussing film history and on national public radio. He lives in San Francisco. His books include:

Curse of the Silver Screen - Tragedy & Disaster Behind the Movies (1999, Aplomb Publishing)

Scare Tactic - The Life and Films of William Castle (2000, Writers Club Press)

Reel Horror - True Horrors Behind Hollywood's Scary Movies (2004, Aplomb Publishing)

Master of Disaster: Irwin Allen - The Disaster Years (2008, Aplomb Publishing)

If you enjoyed this book, you might also enjoy *Master of Disaster: Irwin Allen - The Disaster Years*. Published by Aplomb Publishing, the book is available from our Web site at www.aplomb-publishing.com or from major booksellers and Amazon.com.

www.ingramcontent.com/pod-product-compliance
Lightning Source LLC
Chambersburg PA
CBHW051427290426
44109CB00016B/1464